"Everyone needs a framework as a guide on their personal success journey. No other book provides the complete steps from initial awareness to ultimately mastering your life. In the book, *The Rise of the Chosen Ones: How to Choose Yourself for Greatness,* by Joseph C. Parker, the concepts needed at each level are provided to track your progress."

~**Nadine Lajoie,** Award-Winning Entrepreneur, International Leadership Speaker and Business Mentor http://www.NadineRacing.com

"Are you looking for the fast track to achieving greatness in your life? Joseph C. Parker's book, *The Rise of the Chosen Ones: How to Choose Yourself for Greatness*, is a must read. He gives you practical steps and guidelines for developing the proper mindset so you can shatter your limiting beliefs and achieve the greatness you desire now."

~**Andy Dooley,** Co-founder of TUT.COM and creator of Vibration Activation™

"This book will inspire you to take positive action in your life. Choosing yourself for greatness, instead of waiting to be chosen, will put you on the path to creating your success."

~**Keith Leon,** Multiple Bestselling Author, Publisher, and Motivational Speaker

The Rise Of the Chosen Ones

How to Choose Yourself For Greatness

JOSEPH C. PARKER

Made for Success Publishing
P.O. Box 1775
Issaquah, WA 98027

Library of Congress Cataloging-in-Publication data

Parker, Joseph
The Rise of the Chosen Ones: How to Choose Yourself for
Greatness / Joseph Parker
p. cm.
ISBN-13: 9781613398753 (pbk.)
LCCN: 2016906538

To contact the author or publisher please email service@
MadeforSuccess.net or call +1 425 657 0300.

Made for Success Publishing is an
imprint of Made for Success, inc.

Printed in the United States of America

DEDICATION

To those who seek a more fulfilled life. The mark of true courage is to overcome your mind because the dream you desire can always be yours, if only you will allow yourself to have it.

CONTENTS

Part 1
The Path of the Chosen Ones

Part 2
The Progression of the Chosen Ones

Foreword

In 1961, I was a high-school dropout with a resume of dead-end jobs and a future clouded in debt. But then, I met a man named Ray Stanford who encouraged me to look at the results I was getting, and he handed me a book –*Think and Grow Rich*.

That book and Ray's belief in me planted a seed of hope in my mind. In just months, my life spun on a dime. I was making more than $100,000 in a year and soon topped the $1 million mark.

For the past 55 years, I have focused on helping people create lush lives of prosperity, rewarding relationships, and spiritual awareness. I show people how to understand their hidden abilities to do more, be more and have more in every area of life.

I also read and study every day, and I've noticed something that is missing from most personal success books and courses. Their strategies for success may be sound, but they seldom address the student's lack of belief. However, that's not the case here. In *The Rise of the Chosen Ones: How to Choose Yourself for Greatness*, Joseph Parker reveals a powerful process to create strong self-belief.

Parker begins by describing the myth of the rare chosen one in society. This myth is a compelling story for movies, but it is lousy—and untrue—model for human achievement. It leads people to think that others are more capable and have advantages they do not. It also keeps people stuck in inaction as they wait for someone else to choose them for greatness. Parker explains that everyone must bet on and choose themselves in order to be the star in the movie of their lives.

In part two of the book, Parker reveals a complete set of tools and new psychological models for the personal development process. He makes the transformational process easy to understand and relate to by introducing the concept of levels of attainment. Here's an overview of the attainment levels:

The Initiate: to become aware of your thinking and beliefs, acknowledge your past—and understand how it affected you, and then commit to becoming much more.

The Novice: to choose yourself and accept your greatness. You accept yourself fully with all your flaws and forgive any past mistakes or failures.

The Apprentice: to set your future dreams and adopt a life purpose based on your values. You get to recreate yourself as you always wanted to be.

The Journeyman: to put your dreams into action, you must believe they are possible, and overcome any fears that arise. You learn to seek excellence instead of perfection and have fun along the way.

The Master: to achieve your dreams with gratitude, humility, and to teach others the way. The master is action oriented, free of distractions, and has developed a clear understanding of thoughts and ideas.

Joseph C. Parker has built an impressive resume of helping people improve the quality of their lives. You'll understand why as you dive into the pages of *The Rise of the Chosen Ones: How to Choose Yourself For Greatness* and discover a much-needed roadmap for achieving your dreams and becoming the master of your life.

Bob Proctor

BEGIN

~~~~

INTRODUCTION

Too many people have no belief in their abilities.

T here is a powerful myth that has been handed down throughout the ages. It is the myth of the "chosen one." These rare individuals, supposedly selected for greatness from a higher source, have a destiny to accomplish amazing goals, and they possess knowledge, wisdom, and skills others do not. We see reflections of this myth in classic movies and books such as *Star Wars* and *Harry Potter*.

Great warriors, kings, actors, and athletes are often thought of as Chosen Ones. Indeed, these archetypes do sometimes accomplish amazing deeds, and possess knowledge, power, and skill, but were they really chosen? How did they get to be chosen? Who chose them? How do we access this exclusive club? We will answer these questions and more.

We will discuss and dispel the myth of the chosen one because it is a false belief. Then we will leverage the seductive power of the chosen one myth, for our benefit. By doing this, we will discover that many chosen ones really *do* exist.

However, they are self-made, not appointed by others as the myth describes. We will discover that the deeply personal act of choosing themselves is the psychological key that makes some people great. As we shall see, everyone has the opportunity to become one of the self-chosen ones, and you are able to become one too.

This book shares two powerful, psychological models that contain the core components self-chosen ones will employ for success. You will learn about the seven-part dynamics model, and how it relates to the key concepts matrix. Instructions are provided to assist you in utilizing these models to raise your self-concept, overcome fear walls, and enhance personal beliefs.

The path needed for the journey of the self-chosen ones will be made clear, and the progression levels from Initiate to Master revealed. This framework will guide anyone with the will to be great through the maze of self-improvement concepts. If you choose the path for yourself, the knowledge, actions, and skills required to attain each level is at your fingertips.

This book:

- Dispels the popular "rare chosen one" myth
- Shows how anyone can choose themselves for greatness
- Reveals two psychological models to increase self-concept
- Explains critical core beliefs and strategies for success
- Lays out the path to attaining the master progression level

This book is differs from most as it provides not only personal power concepts, like awareness, belief, and the sub-conscious, but it also provides the necessary business strategies, like intellectual property, "win-win" and conceive-believe-achieve. These concepts are usually kept separate, but in this book, they are interwoven for maximum benefit. Other personal growth books provide development concepts too, but they do not provide a solid set of accompanying business strategies. As a result of providing only concepts without strategies you may charge out, and make many mistakes.

The process of making mistakes can be a good thing because you learn so much from them, however, I want to reduce your learning curve as much as possible upfront to give you the highest probability of future success. The truth is that some strategies work better than others, and you can save yourself years of struggle by knowing what to do and thus, what to avoid. The most successful companies in the world use the business and success strategies in this book. When you adopt them as your own, it will shorten your path to success by up to 10 years, according to the author and visionary Marshall Thurber.

Let us begin by reviewing the current state of the world. Growing up in Western culture has never been easy. Although we live in the wealthiest time and place in the history of mankind, most of us are struggling. Even though there are opportunities all around us, making an adequate living and just getting by is the norm. We see visions of wealth and prosperity on TV, billboards, and on the Internet every day. Images are everywhere of people who have it all. We all want that for ourselves, but somehow the golden rainbow always seems to land on someone else's door.

Why is this? Why is it that in the land of opportunity, so many of us remain disillusioned and broke? Even those who appear to be getting ahead are mostly living beyond their means and worrying about tomorrow. What is it about western culture that lulls people into a deep sleep and allows their lives to pass them by without taking a chance? Why do they continue not to believe in themselves, think themselves undeserving, or not smart enough?

I look around at the culture in which I was raised and see many reasons for this. First, the environment does not support or reward individuality or personal empowerment. Instead, our school system rewards being right, not making mistakes, and social conformity. Second, our media reflects and glorifies being average and poorly behaved. The media networks even encourage bad behavior on reality shows and portray being smart as undesirable and weird.

Third, the environment does not reward taking risks. For example, I sometimes took risks in school that resulted in poor grades or were interpreted as stupid questions. In my school, personal achievement was only measured in regurgitating knowledge, not new learning or creativity. In my high school, being different could result in social obscurity or being an outcast.

Television was my primary media source, and I loved comic book heroes and movie stars who had special skills. My biggest heroes were all mythical chosen ones, such as Spiderman or Superman. Little did I know just how much *that* would hold me back in the future.

Now, a generation later, my sons are growing up in a technical world much different from mine, but still, success is elusive. There are now cell phones, tablets, laptops, watches, and vision goggles that provide 24-7 access to media and entertainment. While these devices make our lives more convenient and useful, they also provide a source of endless distraction and anxiety. The constant stream of music, news, social chatter, and information access has actually made it harder to focus on bettering our lives. How then, can we focus on anything?

The shift created by the Internet and wireless communications has provided youth constant access to media and ideas that few parents can control. Constant negative influences from the media focus on sex, greed, scarcity, and lack of opportunity. Parents are increasingly unable to manage all the demands of modern life and still provide the positive guidance they intended for their children.

What is the result? I believe it is a world in which we now have an epidemic of low self-esteem. This lack of self-esteem has evolved into social and personal problems that are expressed as addiction, distraction, poverty, and consumerism. These problems are actually just self-sabotage and frustration caused by self-loathing. When people have a low self-concept, they engage in activities that expose these negative beliefs such as abusing drugs, alcohol, food, sex, work, and shopping or even turning to violence and crime.

To counteract these problems, we must first address this lack of personal confidence, so that it won't be unleashed in self-defeating behaviors. Too many people have no belief in their own abilities. Too many people blame others for their circumstances. Too many people extract revenge on a society they blame for their problems.

At the root of many social problems are beliefs in myths that are not true. These myths are supported by the media and make us easy to manipulate. On the bright side, once these myths are debunked, the pitfalls they create can be avoided, and one of the biggest myths portrayed to us is that of the rare chosen one. This myth keeps us stuck with no hope of fulfilling our true greater destiny.

Once we escape this myth, we become free to develop ourselves and fulfill our dreams. This takes dedication, skill development, knowledge, and action. When you begin to take action, a path becomes clear, you start to shed fears and doubts, and progressively recreate yourself. Then as one of the new, soon to rise, self-chosen ones, you will need a guide to complete the journey. This book is that guide.

I begin by discussing the historical myth of the chosen one. First, we will review the mythical rare chosen one portrayed in popular movies and literature. Second, we will dispel this myth—these are not true chosen ones because they cannot exist without the missing element that is possessed by real chosen ones—they choose themselves.

Finally, we will show that anyone can become one of the many self-chosen ones. The path these chosen ones take will be made clear, and the core components will be revealed. The psychological frameworks and attainment levels will guide you through the distractions and pitfalls along the journey.

LET'S BEGIN THAT JOURNEY NOW

PART 1

THE PATH OF THE CHOSEN ONES

1

MYTH

THE MYTH OF THE CHOSEN ONE

So why are so many still waiting to be chosen?
We wait for a chance at success or fame hoping to
get that big break by being chosen by others.

Throughout history, we have heard the legendary stories of the mythical chosen one. In these fables, the chosen one is born of or chosen for greatness, success, or adventure. Often, the chosen one is not even aware of their potential until some event forces it to come forward. Then, they rise and fulfill some immense service to the world.

These legends of history are even embodied in religion and ancient books such as the Bible or Aesop's Fables. The Jews were considered the chosen people by some accounts.

It could also be argued that God chose Jesus. There is a lot of choosing going on in these stories, but only for a few.

In more recent times, theater and movies have kept this myth alive. The wizard Harry Potter from the books and movies was recognized as chosen for greatness due to his unknown ability to have seemingly defeated Voldemort. In the story, the great, evil wizard Voldemort came to kill Harry when he was just an infant. Both his parents were killed in the battle, but Voldemort lost almost all of his powers and fled terribly weakened while Harry sustained only a lightning-shaped scar on his head. What a conversation starter the scar must have been.

Luke Skywalker from the movie *Star Wars* was chosen to become a Jedi Knight and save the galaxy from the evil Galactic Empire. According to the movie, after the demise of the Jedi Knights, Luke was chosen by one of the last remaining Jedis to train as one and fulfill his destiny of toppling the evil Empire. Unknown to Luke, his father served the Empire as a Sith. He was certainly born for this job! After many battles, misgivings, and mistakes, Luke becomes a Jedi, and he destroys the dreaded Death Star weapon.

The mythical chosen one is supposedly instilled at birth or by another with special virtues and skills that set them apart from everyone else. Everything then comes naturally to them, and they require little effort to accomplish great tasks. They feel no fear but may initially doubt their abilities. They have intellect and wisdom far above our own. They may not have acquired greatness yet, but it's just a matter of time until they do. How can we all sign up for this job?

Hollywood loves this storyline. In another classic example from 1986, Eddie Murphy starred in the movie *The Golden Child*, which begins in a temple in the distant land of Nepal. Chosen one stories always have an adventure in them. In the story, a young boy has mystical powers and abilities, shows his power to the monks of the temple and, to their amazement, revives a dead bird. Then, to create the movie plot, the boy is captured by some villains and held hostage.

Eddie Murphy, an altruistic and funny social worker in Los Angeles, is contacted by a mysterious Asian woman who tells him of the kidnapping. She says he is the chosen one who will save the child. He does not believe her, although he finds her so attractive he decides to pretend so he can keep her around. He initially doubts his abilities, but soon finds himself on the crazy search for the captors, who for some reason brought the child to Los Angeles.

Ultimately, he finds the courage and strength to save the boy and even win over the beautiful girl. Why does he do this? Did he really need a date that badly? Does he do this because he was the chosen one? Who chose him again? To recap, the Asian woman chose him based upon some divine guidance. And so, true to the chosen one myth, he struggles to believe in his destiny but ultimately prevails.

There are many other movies, which show men and women chosen somehow for greatness. War movies often show soldiers who are chosen to perform a great mission. These men and women usually earn it the hard way. However, the myth often shows examples of people who are able to achieve their goals without hard work, determination, vision, or persistence.

The mythical chosen one achieves their goals by having special abilities, destiny, or luck. They set an unfortunate example for the world that you are either born or chosen for greatness, or you are not. It sounds like a great life, but most of us have not been chosen this way.

Where are the successful movies and stories of the countless men and women who weren't born chosen? Where are the stories of the ones who were born poor, uneducated, disadvantaged, and fearful? Where are the stories of the ones who accomplished amazing things despite their circumstances? We rarely see these types of stories in the popular media. I guess they don't make for compelling movie trailers.

When we see so many mythical chosen one role models, like those shown in *The Golden Child, Star Wars*, and *Harry Potter*, it is little wonder that most don't believe success can happen for them. We are not all a chosen one according to the myth. What if we had better role models showing people of modest means transforming their lives and finding their own greatness? If more role models such as this existed, you would be empowered, inspired, and even motivated. Is there a personal power shortage in most of our lives? I think so.

The examples above show the deception and trap of the chosen one myth. It takes away our personal responsibility and power. It leads us to live in a fantasy world where others control our lives, and we wait for them to make choices for us. It degrades the playing field so that we believe that others have innate abilities and destinies that we cannot share. It distracts us from the true lesson of the mythical chosen one, which will soon be revealed.

Finally, the myth talks of the chosen *one* instead of the chosen *ones*. Aren't we all truly chosen ones? How can the universe love some more than others? In truth, we can all be chosen ones, because nobody possesses wisdom or skill that we do not all share. What we see in popular movies and literature is a farce that teaches us weakness instead of power. It teaches us to rely on outside factors to determine our fate. The mythical chosen one story is truly a myth that holds you back.

There is a fundamental lesson to be learned from these stories if you pay attention to a key issue. What was the common thread that caused Harry Potter, Luke Skywalker, and Eddie Murphy's character in *The Golden Child* to overcome their mediocre lives and accomplish great tasks? Here is a hint: It was not the act of being chosen by someone else. No, even for them being chosen came long before they were able to come into their own power. Being chosen was just a turning point in their lives. It began the journey. It was merely a starting point.

Think of yourself. You know there is huge creativity inside of you waiting to come out. Once you are able to break free from the complacency of waiting, an amazing life will come forth. So why are so many of us still waiting to be chosen? We wait for a chance at success or fame hoping to get that big break from others. To be chosen by an agent, a talent scout, a publishing company, a senior executive, a coach, or a TV show. Is waiting really that much fun?

We have become followers in a very patient world. A world where our patience costs us the loss of our dreams, in exchange for the meager hope of a modest retirement. We distract ourselves on the TV, mobile device, and the Internet to prevent us from noticing the life we missed.

We often wait so long that we fall asleep at the wheel of our lives. Many of us have stopped dreaming and making goals because it's too painful. Dreams are only motivational if we believe we can obtain them. Dreams with little hope of being realized due to their dependence upon others become just reminders of our mediocrity.

So let's understand the myth of the chosen one for what it really is – a poor example of how to succeed. It's an exclusive club that has few members, in fact, no members. Remember; it's a lie that only some of us are chosen. We are all chosen ones. Are you not tired of being lied to?

Let's now move forward and release this myth so that it will no longer have power over us. Then let's examine this myth from another perspective that provides us with power and removes our weaknesses. Your future is bright, and you will soon discover the key that will make you one of the self-chosen ones.

2

$\sim\!\!\sim\!\!\sim$

RISE

THE RISE OF THE CHOSEN ONES

There is a trend in the world and chosen ones are rising up everywhere. They are no longer living by old rules that require them to wait to be recognized by someone else in order to live their dreams.

Let's review again some of the chosen one myth examples that have popularized the concept. In the *Harry Potter* novels and movies, the love and sacrifice of Harry's mother created an unyielding protection for Harry, causing the killing curse to rebound onto Voldemort. This in effect gave Harry some of Voldemort's particular powers, which strengthened as Harry got older and as Voldemort grew stronger. Harry was revered as a living legend and a chosen one. Over the course of his adventures, but not without considerable self-doubt, he finally fulfilled the prophecy that he would vanquish Voldemort.

Luke Skywalker was the son of a fallen Jedi Knight in the *Star Wars* movies. He was a reluctant student of the Force and doubted himself many times along the way. Still, he became a Jedi Knight even after he lost his teacher in a fight with Darth Vader. He resisted the dark side of the Force and fulfilled his destiny by conquering the evil Empire.

In the Eddie Murphy movie *The Golden Child*, he was a man with unlimited potential like all of us. However, he was living below his potential and dealing with his fears and doubts. Does that sound familiar? Suddenly, a mysterious and beautiful Asian woman chooses him for a great deed. This becomes the catalyst that puts him on a journey to discover his inner strength, creativity, and wisdom, which enabled him to overcome the kidnappers and save the boy from danger. Something he could never have imagined doing a few days earlier.

What made the difference for Eddie Murphy in this movie? Is it that he was chosen somehow? No, the act of being chosen just started the process that allowed him to rise above his current situation and become the person inside him waiting to be released. Even though the girl chose him, he still needed to believe in himself to accomplish the tasks required to succeed. It follows then that the real reason for his ultimate success came from eventually choosing himself. When that inner mental and emotional event finally occurred, his inner genius, belief, and confidence were finally released.

Choosing yourself is the missing key lesson from the mythical chosen one story. We must all choose ourselves for greatness before it can ever happen. We must choose ourselves in the same way as someone else would choose us. We must choose our skills, our talents, our knowledge, our bodies with all their flaws and imperfections for success and happiness.

After all, there is no one more qualified and deserving than you.

So what is the ultimate lesson in *The Golden Child* story? Should you wait for a mysterious person to choose you for a secret mission? How long do you think you might wait for this to happen, possibly a lifetime? The truth is that Eddie Murphy's character had the power to choose himself for greatness at any time. He didn't need to wait to be chosen. However, once he made the decision to choose himself for greatness, it was the turning point, and he was able to achieve success.

The same is true for each of us. Many of us wander the world waiting to be chosen for greatness, without realizing our greatness is already in there waiting for us to access it. The act of choosing ourselves is a simple and profound choice. By doing it, we affirm to ourselves, and the world, that our lives are significant, and we have talents and gifts to give. Once we recognize our greatness and make the choice to live to our full potential, we begin to get out of our own way. This is because we are the ones who truly limit ourselves, instead of the greater world around us, as we may assume.

We make excuses for and justify our self-imposed limitations. We say things like, "I could never do that" or, "I am not like that." Each time we justify our limitations we are unconsciously working to keep them in place, which results in driving them deeper into our subconscious mind until we ultimately believe them.

We build an ordinary life of limitation in this way, which results in an ever-shrinking box of restrictions and fear. However, it is a box of our own making, and only we have the key to open it. We do not have to live this way. We can get out of our own way, and shake off these self-imposed limitations. Our fears and limits are only lies we have accepted and allowed to grow in our minds far too long. Like weeds in a garden, we can and must throw them out. We start this process by choosing ourselves for greatness.

Here are affirmations I have found to be powerful. Read them slowly and feel the energy and emotions they create inside you. All change is associated with feelings, and accessing the feelings of power, love, and unlimited potential creates it.

Take time to get in touch with your feelings as you read these:

I choose myself because:

- I have unlimited potential.
- I have gifts to give the world.
- I am no better or worse than others are.
- I have big goals to achieve.
- The world needs strong leaders.
- I am tired of living with less.
- I care about my family.
- I am worth it.
- I am dissatisfied with my current life.
- Nobody else will.

Next, affirm:

- Only I can choose myself.
- Only I can believe in myself.
- Only I can overcome my fears.
- Only I can be confident of my abilities.
- Only I can fulfill my destiny.
- Only I can save the world.

Does the act of choosing yourself provide you with special skills and abilities? In a way, it does because it unlocks your creativity and inner resources. It is a decision point, which provides you with strength and the courage to move towards your goals. It allows you to take responsibility for your life and stop depending on others to save you.

It's important to accept the following thoughts.

Self-Chosen Ones:

- Don't expect things to be easy
- Look to themselves for guidance
- Don't waste time on endless distractions in life
- Do maintain close relationships with their families and friends
- Don't want to fit in
- Stay away from the comfort zone
- Take time to be alone with their thoughts
- Know that failure is the price of success
- Take responsibility for their lives and don't make excuses
- Are honest with themselves and others
- Speak kindly to themselves and others
- Are humble
- Have written goals
- Have extraordinary ideas
- Feel fear, but it doesn't stop them; it attracts them
- Live in faith, not fear.

So chosen ones do exist, but they are not chosen by anyone else. They were not born that way, blessed by God, or given magical powers by a guru. Self-chosen ones are people who believe in themselves and know that they are capable of anything. They see that the world needs leadership, courage, compassion, love, good food, clean water, and wealth. Then, they choose themselves as the best person to accomplish these tasks, utilizing persistence, courage, love, determination, or whatever it takes. They choose to make a difference.

I refer to the mythical chosen one in the singular throughout the book. As you have learned, these people do not actually exist. The chosen ones or the self-chosen ones are referred to in the plural. These are people such as yourself who have decided to take control of their growth and path to greatness. Keep that in mind as you read further.

There is a new trend in the world, and self-chosen ones are rising up everywhere. They are no longer living by old rules that require them to wait to be recognized by someone else to live their dreams. They are taking control of their lives and are not asking for permission from anyone before they take action.

They are living with a higher purpose and commitment and using creativity to make the world a better place. They are shunning the popular media that seeks to keep them in distraction, greed, violence, and fear. They are taking back control of their environment by finding new sources of news and entertainment that support caring, motivation, positivity, and inclusiveness.

The self-chosen ones understand how to bring their superior products and services directly to their customers. They can self-publish their books, music, and movies using the Internet, social media, and mobile devices. They don't need the support of traditional media firms. Self-chosen ones do not allow themselves to be controlled by their devices. Instead, they use them as creation tools not toys for endless distractions.

They understand how to make their offerings unique in the marketplace. They create a tight bond with the clients they serve, so they attract loyal customers. They understand that win-win solutions are always best, and they make sure that any partnership or agreement benefits both parties.

The self-chosen ones take action in the world and are unafraid to make mistakes. They will take the risk to bring their ideas to the world before they are completely ready, making adjustments and improvements as they go. When mistakes are made, they understand this is good feedback on how to deliver better service. They accept mistakes as the best way to learn anything and know they are not a reflection of anyone's character or value. In fact, they are eager to learn from their mistakes and find new ways to improve themselves and their positive work in the world.

Self-chosen ones live by their values and higher purpose and use those values to evaluate every decision they make. They are doing something every day to bring their visions to life. They have given up pleasing others and instead do things that please themselves and their higher purpose. They accept the things in life they are unable to change and know that self-love is the way to happiness.

The modern world is hungry for more self-chosen ones. The stage is set for their success. They will become the world leaders who will reverse the course of violence, greed, hunger, fear, and oppression in the world. There is no better time than now. You are one of the new self-chosen ones.

3

~~~~~~

CHOSEN?

ARE YOU ONE OF THE CHOSEN ONES?

*I am one of the chosen ones! I don't
need anyone else to choose me.*

Have you noticed how many chosen one themed movies there are? The silver screen is flooded with heroes, kings, queens and masked marvels. We enjoy chosen one myth movies; I believe because we all want to be chosen for greatness from humble means. The stories help us imagine a future where we become special and powerful, one where we can transform into the person we wish to become.

Many of us wait for the opportunity to be chosen. We wait for a job promotion, or to be accepted into a management-training program. We wait to be selected for the acting part that will launch our performance career or for a leading role in our lives instead of supporting others dreams and goals. We wait for that great business idea, for the stock market to change, or for the economy to improve. We wait to be selected to sing or act on *The Voice*, a reality show, or *America's Got Talent*. We simply wait and wait for others and outside events to choose us.

- Why do we wait? You don't need anyone's permission to begin.
- What if you didn't have to wait? Because you don't.
- What if you already had that greatness inside of you? You do, you know.
- What if the world was waiting for you to choose yourself instead? Because…it is!

The truth is we don't have to wait for others or events to choose us for anything. All the great minds that came before us chose themselves first as leaders. Therefore, we are all free to choose ourselves for greatness at any time. True personal greatness never comes from the outside. It comes from an inner decision that recognizes our own leadership, talents, and abilities. We dismiss the negative thoughts we have allowed to hold us back, and release the judgments of others and ourselves. In addition, and most importantly, we forgive others and ourselves for the past.

We make a conscious and real decision to change our lives. Did you know a real decision has only one possible outcome? Can you make a real decision that you will not go back to your old ways of thinking? Make a decision that embraces the only possible outcome where you hold yourself accountable and overcome the past limitations on your capabilities. When made, this type of bold, real decision becomes a turning point in your life. Remember you have no limits and fear is an illusion.

In my life, I have made many decisions that displayed that I chose myself for greatness. In one example, I applied for a leadership development program at work. The two-year leadership program had a history of producing promotions and future leaders. I took great care to ensure my application and recommendations were stellar, and I was confident I would be accepted.

Although I interviewed well, I did not get into the highly competitive program. My reaction could have been depression and loss of self-confidence. I might have believed it meant something negative about me, stopped working so hard on my job, and accepted my fate. Instead, using my own funds, I chose another path and enrolled myself in a leadership program outside of my company. The first class was $495, a significant investment in my self-growth. Since graduating from college, I had made few investments in myself. This was a new beginning for me.

The result of that initial investment in my personal growth has been profound. It started me on a course of development that has taken me farther than anyone who was accepted to the company leadership program. The awareness training helped me to focus on how to think instead of what to think, and I received a job promotion within months of starting my leadership program.

I used to think that knowledge is power. However, I have discovered that knowledge alone is not power. Power comes through action, and most training classes and schools focus only on knowledge. I now understand knowledge must be paired with ability, confidence, vision, and action.

My personal leadership program is focused on unlocking my self-confidence, creating a vision, and enabling me to take action on the knowledge and skills I already possess. The job promotion was just the beginning of a series of incredible events that have been unfolding in my life and my wife's since we chose ourselves for greatness.

I started an Internet radio stationed called Program Your Life (PYL) Radio. I created the PYL podcast, which I host with my wife. I became an author. My wife has written her own dramatic play about hearing loss and acts as the solo performer and star. She is also creating a workshop and will soon be a speaker.

Here is what I have come to understand.

Self-Chosen Ones:

- Are active creators of their lives instead of bystanders waiting for outside events to occur
- Do not hope for luck to smile upon them
- Know luck is for those who have no plan
- Pursue their dreams one step at a time and do not need to know the outcome
- Strive for excellence and not perfection
- Stay in movement towards their goals and accept the opportunities that arrive along the way
- Focus their minds on what they want
- Do not accept well-intentioned but limiting advice from others
- Do not makeup stories about what others are thinking about them
- Like to be different. They do not want to fit in
- Have a daily routine of caring for themselves through exercise and meditation
- Always look for win-win solutions
- Want the world to be a better place and find ways to make it happen.

Do you want to be one of the self-chosen ones? It's an easy process to begin the journey, and there is a path to guide you along the way. It takes a single step to start the process. This single step, if taken seriously, will launch you on a new path in your life. Don't wait to do it, or for someone else to do it for you.

Choose yourself to have a successful and happy life. Choose yourself to be an author, singer, musician, poet, businessperson, speaker, coach, leader, or teacher. Become one of the self-chosen ones by choosing yourself. Say the sentence below aloud if you are ready to become a chosen one.

I am one of the chosen ones! I don't need anyone else to choose me. I am extraordinary, and I matter. I can change the world. I choose myself for greatness! I will wait no longer!

This process is how you will create your power in the world, and release yourself from the need to be chosen. This is your time and your hour and the turning point in your life. You now have been chosen for great deeds and accomplishments by choosing yourself.

Notice how it feels to choose yourself. Did you get a warm or cool feeling in your chest or face? This is how being one of the self-chosen ones feels. You can give this to yourself at any time. Repeat the phrase above again or say the affirmations in the last chapter to regain this feeling.

Write this mantra down, place it on your bathroom mirror, and say it every morning. Do this each day before you go into the world to feel your true worth. The world has been waiting for you to take your rightful place as a leader. You are now a leader of self and others. When you lead yourself, others will follow.

To become a master self-chosen one you not only need to choose yourself, but you need to believe in yourself. To do this, you may need to perform a form of mental judo. This is truly the hardest part. It is what is missing from the Law of Attraction, and many other personal development programs. We will use mental judo to uproot the old limiting beliefs about yourself and implant new ideas and beliefs about what is possible for you.

The old you probably lived in a box or a comfort zone. The box was built to protect you from the world and others. This box served its purpose while you were maturing, but now it may have become a prison that holds you in fear and bondage. The box often contains beliefs that have never been true such as "I'm not enough," or "I'm not smart," or "People need to like me." In our youth, we decided or agreed these things were true and then looked out into the world for evidence of their existence. We found this evidence or we created it so that we could be right about our beliefs. The human need to be right is unyielding even if it holds us back.

The reality is we could have made very different positive choices about our beliefs, such as, "I am enough," or "I'm smart," or "People's opinions of me are none of my business." Unbelievably, once these different choices are made, we'll find just as much evidence that they, too, are true. You see, we mentally filter the world based on our beliefs and our filters always will bring back evidence of what we believe.

Think of our mental filters as a Google search engine. When we search the world for our beliefs using Google as a mind filter, it will always bring back results. We use these results as evidence of our beliefs. However, if we were to search for other, more positive, beliefs these too would bring back just as many results. In this way, what we believe about ourselves is always true because we make it so. For this reason, be careful what you choose to believe, and I suggest you make your beliefs awesome. Let us now begin the process of changing old limiting beliefs.

The mental judo required to overcome our limitations is a form of reprogramming our minds. According to Bob Proctor, from the documentary *The Secret*, our minds have two parts: the conscious and subconscious. The conscious mind does all our rational thinking, learns things, and occasionally transfers knowledge and beliefs to the subconscious mind for future use. In the conscious mind, we create our goals and visions, and we control our body, that is until our mind becomes preoccupied. As our mind starts to drift out of the present moment and into the future or past, the subconscious mind takes over, and we go into a form of autopilot.

The autopilot in your subconscious mind has been developing or programming itself over your lifetime. The conscious mind learns things or creates beliefs and then it transferred them to the subconscious mind for later use. For example, the process of tying a shoe needed to be learned at first, but once it was successfully transferred to the subconscious mind, you no longer had to think about it. Your fingers just performed the behavior using this beneficial mental program. It became automatic because you programmed yourself to do it.

On the contrary, sometimes these automatic tasks performed by the subconscious mind can end up controlling us. For example, suppose you are on your way home from work or going to a place you know very well. You decide ahead of time to take a detour or stop along the way, but as you arrive, you find that you missed the turn to take the detour and have arrived at the place you know well instead. How did you forget to make the stop? It happened because your conscious mind got preoccupied with something else allowing your subconscious mind to take over and complete a program it understands well. Your subconscious mind took control of your behavior.

This also can happen after you decide to become one of the self-chosen ones. Your conscious mind decides and is ready to make the changes. You have chosen yourself, set values, goals, and created a vision. You are ready to take action in alignment with your higher purpose, but then your mind gets preoccupied with something else. A random thought demands your attention or you take a mental break.

Instantly, your subconscious mind takes over and runs an old ingrained program that says, "I'm not enough" or "What will other people think?" Your subconscious mind has not yet received your new thoughts and beliefs and is still working to keep you in the box. You begin to feel change is too difficult. This is when applying mental judo is required.

Some of our mental programs are no longer beneficial to us. They need to be replaced, and the process is not easy. The negative programs have been in place a long time and may even be reinforced on a daily basis due to our environment or habits. For example, fear is a tough program to change. A few fears are rational, but most fears that stop people from action are an illusion.

If you are in the habit of watching TV news, then you are being spoon-fed a constant stream of fear and examples of violence. This will add to your fears or reinforce them. Making changes to your daily habits and even who you spend time with may be necessary.

Some people have developed a very negative outlook on life and complain about almost everything. They act like victims who are at the mercy of the economy, the government, their employers, or other people. They will spread their fears and doubts to everyone around them. Being in their presence is toxic to a self-chosen one.

If you have one or more of these people in your life, then action is required. You cannot change them. They can only change themselves. You must separate yourself from them and find positive minded people for friends or spouses. If you are married to one of these people, your road ahead will be even more difficult. The key here is to identify and hopefully to remove any environmental factors that are reinforcing negative beliefs and programs.

Your mental judo goal is to keep your conscious mind filled with new positive thoughts and ideas about yourself for as long as possible. Reinforce those ideas by looking for evidence of them in the real world. Meditate on those thoughts and repeat your mantra as often as possible. The longer you do this, the more you will transfer these beliefs to your subconscious mind. This process takes time and effort.

You will also want to create a positive environment for yourself to expedite the transfer of beneficial beliefs about the world and yourself to the subconscious mind. Here is what I suggest: stop watching the TV news or reading the details of all the horrors of the world. Feeding yourself a stream of what's wrong with the world will only keep you thinking negatively. If you must keep up with world events, just read the headlines or stick to articles and topics that make you feel good.

Stay away from TV programs and video games that display or glorify violence. Violence in our world is not going to stop while we continue to support it with products or TV shows that display it in graphic detail. Violence only creates fear and fear is a dream killer.

Lastly, you cannot obtain your dreams until you confront the fear walls that block your course. Fear walls are the edges of your comfort zone. As you expand your thoughts and take action towards your goals, you will hit many fear walls. It takes courage to push through them and obtain the rewards in accomplishments, belief, and confidence. Each time you push through a fear wall, your ability to do so becomes stronger.

4

~~~

BELIEVE

THE DYNAMICS MODEL

*To develop your unstoppable personal belief, you
will leverage the power of the planets in your
solar system beginning with your own star.*

N ow that you have declared yourself one of the self-
chosen ones, you are in an exclusive group. Most
people are still hoping to be chosen and are waiting
for something outside of themselves to start their dreams in
to motion. There is no more time to waste on waiting. Your
decision to choose yourself allows you to move forward and
take action on your goals. This is true empowerment.

This chapter holds a framework you can use to understand
the critical elements self-chosen ones use to obtain their
dreams and become their best selves. This is provided
because it is important to have a structured path to track your

progress and growth. Just follow the path and your grand destiny awaits. In the next chapter, the chosen one's levels of attainment will be discussed.

During my research into personal development, I discovered there is a dynamics model that contains all the critical elements that fully-actualized chosen ones possess. You can think of the Dynamics Model as a set of planets orbiting an inner solar system. This solar system exists at the metaphysical layer inside your mind, and it helps us understand how the development concepts interrelate.

The seven elements of the chosen one's Dynamics Model are:

- Believe in yourself
- Create yourself
- Infinite intelligence
- Strategies
- Habits
- Characteristics
- Environment

At the center of the dynamics model is the sun or star of your solar system. This is where all the heat, love, desire, belief, and energy come from that power your dreams, transforms your health and sustain your relationships. The star at the center of your solar system is the most critical element. All the other objects revolving in this system are there to support it and are utilized for transforming your life. This is where the mental judo of belief is applied, and its results made evident.

Around the star of your solar system are six orbiting planets that contain the building blocks and tools used to transform your life. Each of these planets has a special purpose, and together they keep the entire system in balance and harmony. Growth in all these spheres is required to bring your life's vision into existence. Ignoring a single planet's growth can throw the entire solar system out of alignment. Your task is to grow your entire solar system into an ever-expanding galaxy. The larger your solar system becomes, the closer you are to your dreams and goals.

Each of these elements has many subcomponents that will be explained later. Table 1 shows the inner solar system of the self-chosen ones. At its center is the heat source: Believe in yourself. This is the most critical of all elements. The orbiting planets bring balance to the system and support this belief as well as act as tools for goal achievement. The planets are of equal importance to each other and are collectively necessary for the system to function in harmony.

Table 1 – The Chosen One's Dynamics Model

After you observe the overall model, you will discover that each element has subcomponents. The subcomponents are concepts to be understood or actions to take that expand your solar system and move you upward through the hierarchy of the chosen one's path. Each is a skill, habit, strategy, or thought process to be mastered during the journey toward your vision. As you learn, you may discover you are already strong in some areas and perhaps weak in others. This provides feedback to help you decide where best to apply your efforts.

As mentioned earlier, at the center of your solar system is your star, which indicates your belief in yourself. Note it is rarely possible to work solely and directly on belief in yourself to the exclusion of other solar system elements. Without the planets of your solar system to support your belief, there can be no progress towards goals, action, or obtainment. Becoming a master self-chosen one requires action. This is not something you can obtain from a mental or meditative state. Enlightenment of the mind must be mirrored into the world for completeness; moreover, the world needs the gifts you will bring forth.

To develop an unstoppable personal belief, you leverage the power of the planets in your solar system, but you begin with your star. To expand the belief inside your star, there are a few steps and it starts with choosing yourself for greatness. Then, you proceed to believe your dreams are possible for you, overcoming your fear walls, not caring what others think, expanding your self-concept, and then reprograming your subconscious mind. Belief in yourself must be mastered because low self-esteem can sabotage any dream or goal.

Your star is at the center of the model and larger than the other planets because of its importance in the process. It is true; you are who you believe you are, and you will receive what you think you deserve. Raising your belief in yourself is the key factor in all personal growth.

The planets in the model will manifest into the real world what you believe in your mind. There are six planets that revolve around the star of belief and we will explore them next.

The "Create Yourself" planet gives you the opportunity to create and recreate yourself. Your past does not define your future. Therefore, you can recreate yourself at any time. You do this by setting new goals, choosing values, and connecting with a higher purpose. As you pursue ever bigger goals, you are constantly renewing who you are and what you believe.

In the chapters that follow, you will be given a chance to redefine your values, learn to live for yourself and not others, improve your relationships, live more healthy, and decide what you want. Ultimately, you will identify and embrace your higher purpose.

The "Infinite Intelligence" planet is your door to accessing the superconscious because everything you need to know is already available in the universe once you get connected to it. By using meditation and clear thinking, you learn to access unlimited creativity and knowledge. Getting in touch with the feelings of obtaining your dreams is used to help make them possible. You will also learn to live with faith of positive outcomes rather than being controlled by fear of failure.

The "Habits" planet is devoted to developing effective and supportive habits and routines. These habits will make you outwardly focused, willing to be inconvenienced, become a true giver, and seek excellence instead of perfection. You will learn how to remove distractions, take time for yourself, stop making up stories, overcome the comfort zone, have fun, and exercise along the way.

Your daily habits and routines are very important. These repetitive activities are similar to setting a ship's course. Habits projected out across your lifetime dictate where you will arrive in the future and making small corrections to habits can vastly change your future when accumulated over a lifetime. Some habits will lead to success, others to failure.

The "Characteristics" planet holds all the personal traits you want to embody. You begin by increasing your personal awareness and then move on to gratefulness, forgiveness, acceptance, responsibility, and persistence. You will learn how to stop being hard on yourself, which is an unhealthy characteristic that punishes us for past mistakes. Instead, by adopting acceptance, you learn to release your critical self-judgments and find forgiveness.

Once you are free of your past habits and beliefs, you begin to employ the "Strategies" planet; it contains proven strategies for wealth and happiness. These are very effective for self-chosen ones who have learned to get out of their own way. These strategies include a three-step process for success: how to take action, how to employ leverage, and how staying in motion leads to your true purpose. They also teach how to manage distractions, learn from mistakes, utilize teams, and how intellectual property dominates as a business strategy.

Strategies are crucial to individual success but can be overemphasized. For example, for many years, I believed that good strategies were all I needed. I thought knowledge alone was enough. It was years later that I discovered that my personal beliefs had sabotaged every effort I undertook. Once I changed my beliefs, the strategies became effective.

The final "Environment" planet helps you stay focused on the journey as you learn how to restructure and control your environment for success. It covers removing negative influences, seeking out other self-chosen ones, and, on a daily basis, adding sources of positive inspiration in your life. You will also learn to avoid violent images so that your fertile mind can grow the types of ideas and thoughts you desire.

Your environment either assists in your progress or detracts from it. You will learn to identify and remove negative reminders of your past. Clearing out and releasing old objects and ideas creates room to acquire new positive ideas, items, and clothes about which you feel great. You will learn to feed your mind with positive information and avoid negative sources of news and ideas.

In the next chapter, self-chosen one levels of attainment are discussed. Then, in part two of the book, we go into detail about concepts within each attainment level. Some concepts are more important in the beginning, and some become more critical at higher levels. This breaks up the material and focuses learning only on what is needed at each stage. As you grow, additional topics are introduced as needed. All together this process is a highly structured system of growth and achievement.

We will review the Dynamics Model again in a coming chapter as part of the Key Concepts Matrix. This is a handy new way to approach the topics, show a hierarchy, and observe how they fit together. In part two of the book, we will discuss the progression of the chosen ones.

5

~~~~~~

ATTAIN

THE LEVELS OF ATTAINMENT

What should you do first and when do you shift from self-reflection to acceptance, creation, and then into action?

One of the problems with most personal improvement books and courses is that they are unable to provide the individual with a reliable road map or even a way of gauging their progress towards mastering the concepts. Each book focuses only on certain topics, and they are never fully integrated into an overall framework with simple progression levels.

The progression levels defined here are a useful way to gauge individual progress along the path of personal development. They are meant to be used as milestones on the journey and not for recognition of achievement. This book divides the journey of the self-chosen ones into five distinct levels that everyone will pass through on the way to obtaining their dreams.

This is important because without a framework many people flounder, do not know where to focus, or understand how the concepts build upon each other. For example, one book may talk about forgiveness or awareness and another one will focus on goals or action. What should you do first and when do you shift from self-reflection to acceptance, creation, and then into action?

Gratitude Subconscious
Responsibility Values
Win-win
Exercise Diversity
Persistence Fear
Belief Leverage Health
Vision
Meditation Faith
Forgiveness Action
Relationships Creativity
Distractions Acceptance
Comfort zone

How do you know when you have built a firm mental and emotional foundation to build your dreams? When do you use each planet in your solar system? It can be very confusing, and you can quickly become overwhelmed with too much information and too many questions. This is where the organized path provided in the following chapters of this book is needed.

The chosen one levels of attainment again are milestones along the path. Each level has a distinct purpose, knowledgebase, and a set of goals. Each level also requires that you use a different set of the personal growth concepts that are part of your solar system. Some of these concepts are used more than others at each level. For example, persistence becomes more important as you move up each level. Consider Table 2 as a reference.

Table 2 – Self-Chosen Levels

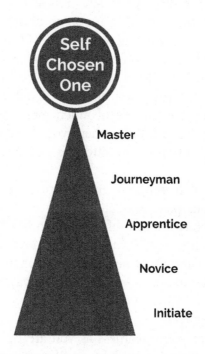

The levels are a hierarchy that represents your progression as one of the self-chosen ones. They show your proficiency and are set up like a trade guild or martial arts system with levels. The names given for each level are loosely based upon the medieval guild system. I have added more levels to make five.

As a reference, the guilds were associations of skilled workers who went through a lifetime progression to become a master at their craft. The names are used differently here and are not meant to align with the actual guild levels.

Everyone who chooses themselves starts as an Initiate. This is where you begin awareness training. Awareness training entails discovering how your mind works and how your mental programs often control you. You will also examine your past and how you became who you are now. The influences of others are very strong here. You will begin to identify your beliefs about yourself, define areas for improvement and then commit to living in a new way. You will cast aside the need to fit in and begin to accept your uniqueness.

The initiate level has a purpose: to become aware, acknowledge your past and how it affected you, and then realize you are capable of much more. You will know you are ready to advance when you have defined areas for improvement and committed, as never before, to overcome them.

Next you progress to Novice where you completely accept your past, evaluate your present circumstances, take responsibility for your life, and choose yourself for greatness. You will choose your values and remove negative influences. You will learn about negative story making and how it leads to fear. Meditation is introduced as a way to think clearly and relax.

The purpose of the novice level is to choose yourself and accept your greatness as you are right now. You accept yourself with all your flaws and forgive any past mistakes or failures. You will evaluate your health and focus on making it better. The high price of being normal will be made clear.

As an Apprentice, you get to set new goals for your life and recreate yourself as if you were ordering your life from a menu where there are no limits. Your beliefs about yourself will begin to change. You will become grateful for what you already have, and learn to forgive others and yourself.

Mistakes will no longer be considered as negative. They will be encouraged as part of your new learning process.

The purpose of the apprentice level is to set your future goals and create a life purpose based on your values. You will recreate yourself as you always wanted to be. You will transform your environment, learn business strategies, and learn to live in faith instead of fear. You will know you are ready to advance to the next level when you have decided what you want, set goals to achieve it, defined a higher purpose, come to believe it is possible for you, and accepted that inconvenience is the price of success.

Then, you move to a Journeyman, which is about belief and becoming action oriented. Here you put your goals into action steps, use strategies, and begin to overcome your fear walls. You will develop persistence as you take action towards your goals. You will act with responsibility and find like-minded others to join your efforts. You will employ strategies such as win-win, distraction management, and intellectual property.

The purpose of the journeymen level is to put your goals into action, believe they are possible, and overcome the fears that stand in your way. You will learn to seek excellence instead of perfection and have fun along the way. You will learn to connect with infinite intelligence and absorb the knowledge of the universe. Overcoming negative story making will make all the difference. You will know you are ready to advance to the next level once you have based your goals upon a higher purpose and made them a reality.

Ultimately, you want to become a Master. The master knows how to create a vision and see it achieved through action, belief, creativity, flexibility, and persistence. The master also lives for a higher purpose. The master has high self-value and self-esteem. They have an indifference to others opinions of them. They are grateful for everything and take total responsibility for all that happens. They understand what it takes to achieve a vision.

The purpose of the master level is to achieve your visions with gratitude, humility, and to teach others the way. The master is action oriented, free of distractions, and has a clear understanding of their thoughts and emotions. They are very exclusive in their selection of outside influences including people and information. They find joy in everyone and are guided by faith.

Consider again the diagram previously shown in table 2. This is your roadmap to becoming a master chosen one. In the next chapter, we will blend the dynamics model and levels of attainment together. This provides a systematic program for personal development mastery, and the process of life success will be demystified.

6

THE KEY

THE KEY CONCEPTS MATRIX

*What is it I believe about myself that is
untrue and is holding me back?*

The Dynamics Model, from a previous chapter, provides a framework to understand the importance of self-esteem and how the self-chosen one elements interrelate. As you learned, it is similar to a solar system, with your core beliefs at its center. Its true power lies in what you believe about yourself.

The Attainment Levels, from the last chapter, are a hierarchy of personal development concepts that move through the stages of awareness, forgiveness, learning, creating, and achievement. The higher you go in the levels, the more powerful you become. Separately, these two models are significant new ways of understanding and placing structure around self-growth, but there is more. As an even further refinement, the chosen one's Attainment Levels and the Dynamics Model can be combined into the Key Concepts Matrix.

Table 3 – Key Concepts Matrix (condensed version)

Level	Purpose	Believe in Yourself	Create Yourself	Habits	Strategies	The Infinite	Environment	Characteristics
Master	Achieve your vision with gratitude	High Self-value indifferent to other opinions	Vision achievement	Clarity of thought Fond joy in everything	Distraction mastery Action oriented	Guidance by faith	Exclusive influences	Gratitude in all things Total responsibility
Journeyman	Put goals into action and overcome fear	Overcome fear walls. Live outside comfort zone	Progress towards vision	Have Fun Distraction mgmt. Seel excellence	Apply win-win Learning from mistakes intellectual property	Infinite Intelligence Feeling of success	Interact with like-minded others	Persistence Act with Responsibility
Apprentice	Set future goals and life purpose based on values	Believe in self. Increase self-value	Decide what you want. Higher purpose	Allow inconvenience Have fun	Conceive-Believe-Achieve Encourage mistakes	Live in faith not fear Meditation-Creativity	Transform your environment	Become Grateful Forgiveness
Novice	Choose yourself and accept your greatness in the present	Choose yourself	Choose your values	Stop story making	Health evaluation	Meditation walking	Remove negativity Mend relationships	Forgive yourself Responsibility
Initiate	Become aware and acknowledge the past	Subconscious mind	Commit to change	Identify Habits	Identify Beliefs	Awareness of the universe	Evaluate the present	Awareness of self

The Key Concepts Matrix provides a system that integrates the five attainment levels with the seven elements of the dynamics model. The key concepts listed in each cross section become more advanced as you move up the levels. This useful framework can be used to track your progress along the journey to becoming a master.

The Key Concepts Matrix places the attainment levels on the vertical axis. You will see that more advanced concepts and skills are introduced as you move up levels. The dynamics model's seven elements are displayed on the horizontal axis. Listed in each cross-section box are the major concepts and actions that must be mastered to advance.

As you review the Key Concepts Matrix, you will find it contains the mindset, skills, abilities, beliefs, characteristics, environments, and strategies needed to become a master in all areas of life. At each level, you only need to concentrate on the concepts listed and fulfill the purpose of moving forward

The key concepts matrix in this book shows only a summary of the concepts in each cross section box. A complete listing of all the elements in the concepts matrix is too large to be shown in this book. If you would like to obtain a FREE complete matrix, please go to my website.

http://www.riseofthechosenones.com/matrix

To use the matrix for your success, start at the bottom row and read the purpose of the initiate level, which is to "become aware and acknowledge the past." This is the goal of the first level. Here you will look at your past and understand how it affected your development.

On this bottom row are columns with the concepts and activities to be accomplished or learned by the initiate before moving forward. One of the first elements is the subconscious mind. This row is all you need to focus upon to get started. You need not worry about the other higher concepts yet. The initiate chapter will walk you through the first level elements and let you know when you are ready to advance.

Once you advance to a novice, you will have a whole new purpose and set of concepts and activities to accomplish. As a novice, you get to choose yourself for greatness, forgive yourself, and accept the ways you are unique. The elements of that row support this purpose and provide tools to help you commit to a better life. These elements build on the initiate level. The novice chapter will guide you through this process and provide advancement criteria.

At level three as an apprentice, your purpose changes to "set future goals and your life's higher purpose based on your values." Here you will recreate yourself with new objectives and a higher purpose. All the planetary elements in that row from the dynamics model again support this purpose. You will also notice that the number of elements is increasing, and they are more advanced skills and beliefs. It is a building process tailored to your individual needs.

The journeyman at level four is the action level. Your purpose here is working towards your goals, changing your beliefs, and overcoming fears. The business strategies now come into play; your self-concept has risen, and you discover that mistakes and doubts can no longer stop you. You now realize that mistakes are for learning and mean nothing about your self-worth. The journeymen chapter will present the elements needed and how to advance.

The top row of the matrix is the master level. There is still much to learn here. Your purpose becomes to complete your goals, find gratitude, give back, and take total responsibility for your life. The elements of this top row support you, and the chapter takes you through the process. By now, your vibration is at a very high level, and others will seek you out as a teacher. You will want to reach out to those who are ready and lift then up with knowledge and support.

It is a very select person that can develop themselves in all these areas and become a grand master self-chosen one. This is your goal and once you achieve it harmony, balance, and peace of mind will be yours. You will continue to evolve the vision of your life and have the mindset, knowledge, and beliefs to do anything you wish. You have become a master self-chosen one.

When reviewing the matrix, you may observe people who appear to have become masters by focusing on only a few vertical concepts. It is true; you can be great in only one or two areas and become a very powerful person. Beware, because these types of focused masters have vulnerabilities in areas they have not yet mastered. They must be cautious because a weakness in a single area can completely sabotage their future.

There are many examples of people who mastered a single focused area of their lives and were able to thrive for a while.

Unfortunately, the neglected areas were weaknesses that others could easily exploit. There have been some very public examples of famous people who have fallen from grace due to weaknesses in gambling, sex, drugs, and illegal behavior. Professional athletes are prime examples of this.

Here are some examples of a focused master. Entertainers and performers are often just masters of the Belief and Creation columns. Priests and preachers have become masters of the Infinite Intelligence and Habits columns. Wealthy business people have become masters of the Strategies and Characteristics columns. Keep in mind, all of these focused masters must also be masters of their beliefs.

Examples of grand masters are fewer but are more impressive. These people have taken the time to focus on their inner world, change their thinking, and then make it consistent with their outer world. A few names that would probably make the list include Gandhi, Nelson Mandela, Mother Teresa, Abraham Lincoln, Dr. Martin Luther King, and the Dalai Lama.

These people overcame their fears, fought hard for their dreams, took huge risks, and were action oriented. They were masters in all the chosen one dynamics as well as the levels. Most of all, they chose themselves as the best person to perform the tasks to be done. They believed what they wanted was possible. They believed in themselves and their abilities.

Remember, if you cannot master your belief system and self-concept, then mastery in all other areas will not be enough. The lack of belief in yourself will ultimately sabotage any efforts that you undertake. This cannot be overlooked or underemphasized. Your beliefs are omnipresent.

The next five chapters will describe each attainment level in detail along with what strategies, characteristics, and skills are required to move forward. You will find that many concepts build upon each other and that there is a time and place for their use.

Underlying all these levels and constantly in the center of your solar system, will remain your personal beliefs and self-concept. Each level will both build your self-concept and require that you display it through the steps you take. If you find that you are having difficulty at any level, or with any step, return to your personal beliefs.

Ask yourself this question: what is it I believe about myself that is untrue and is holding me back? If you return to this question and directly confront the mistaken beliefs each time you struggle, the path can be cleared just by shifting your beliefs. It is never the world which limits us; it is our limited beliefs which hold us back.

To move forward towards mastery as a self-chosen one, you must overcome the limits of your mind. The battle in our minds is always greater than the battle outside. As my wife Kimberly says, "It's an inside job."

7

QUIZ

THE CHOSEN ONE QUIZ

*Knowledge alone is not power. Power is
knowledge combined with belief and action.*

Before we begin exploring the progression levels of
the self-chosen one; it's time for a fun quiz. I have
prepared a wholly unscientific quiz to gauge patterns
of thinking and how they affect your outlook on life. Since you
have gotten this far in the book, you're obviously someone
who wants to learn a better way.

The quiz below is also available on my website. Let's have
some fun and discover your degree of understanding of the
five levels on the path. This will give you a general sense of
your awareness and current personal growth mindset. It does
not gauge accomplishment or the actionable use of these
ideas which are critical to success.

Regardless of where you score academically, you will want to go through all five levels of the self-chosen one. This is because knowledge of a concept is not the same as doing the work to implement it in your life. Remember knowledge alone is not power. Power is knowledge combined with belief and action. My answers to this quiz are listed in the back of the book in the Appendix.

CHOSEN ONE QUIZ

When taking the quiz, remember to choose the answer that fits the person you are now, not as you want to be. Choose one answer for each question below.

S – Choose the sentence that best describes you now
1. Success is inconvenient
2. Success is in my future
3. Success takes commitment and work
4. Success is easy for me

W – Choose the sentence that best describes you now
1. Other people deserve my best
2. I talk kindly to myself
3. I hold myself to a high personal standard
4. I am always doing better

P – Choose the sentence that best describes you now
1. I am always getting better
2. I always strive to be my very best
3. People deserve only my best
4. I cannot always do my best

C – Choose the sentence that best describes you now
1. I like others to like me
2. I like to be different than everyone else
3. I like to be the life of the party
4. I like to be accepted by my peers

M – Choose the sentence that best describes you now
1. It's important to visualize the end
2. It's important to take steps
3. It's important to stay focused
4. It's important to make sure I have the correct goal

R – Choose the sentence that best describes you now
1. My choices are mostly good
2. I am like my parents
3. I am not a product of my environment
4. My environment has strongly shaped my life

G – Choose the sentence that best describes you now
1. I forgive but do not forget
2. I protect myself from others who have hurt me
3. I forgive, so others feel better
4. I forgive so I feel better

M – Choose the sentence that best describes you now
1. I proceed carefully to do things correctly
2. I like to make mistakes
3. I make decisions quickly and occasionally fail
4. I like to avoid mistakes

S – Choose the sentence that best describes you now
1. I can usually tell what others think
2. I anticipate what others think about me
3. I don't know what others think
4. I can sometimes tell what others think

L- Choose the sentence that best describes you now
1. I am a leader of others
2. I prefer to follow a strong leader
3. I am a leader of myself
4. I am a reluctant leader

I – Choose the sentence that best describes you now
1. I like to tie
2. I don't mind to lose
3. I like to win
4. I like to cooperate

V – Choose the sentence that best describes you now
1. I believe that other's needs are more important than mine
2. I believe my needs are equal to others
3. I believe my needs must be met before considering other's needs
4. I believe that my needs are more important than others

F – Choose the sentence that best describes you now
1. Few fears are rational
2. Fear is a necessary part of life
3. I prefer not to fear
4. There is no fear

E – Choose the sentence that best describes you now
1. I exercise when it's convenient
2. I exercise on a calendar schedule
3. I exercise rarely
4. I exercise to feel better about myself

HOW TO SCORE YOUR QUIZ

Each question had four possible answers, so the table below has four columns. For each question circle the number in the column that corresponds to the number of the answer you picked. For example, if you picked answer number 1 for the first question on success, go to column 1 on the first row below and circle the 2. This is because you get 2 points for choosing number 1 for this question.

If you picked answer 1 for the second question, you would circle the zero in the second row of column 1. Do this process for each question. There should only be one circled number for each row. Then add up the circled numbers in each column to determine your total score.

Answers	1	2	3	4
S - Success	2	0	0	1
W – Hard on Self	0	2	0	1
P - Perfection	2	0	0	1
C - Independence	0	2	0	0
M – In Motion	1	2	0	0
R - Environment	1	0	2	0
G - Forgiveness	0	0	1	2
M - Mistakes	0	2	1	0
S – Make up Stories	0	0	2	1
L - Leadership	1	0	2	0
I – Win-Win	1	0	0	2
V – Self Value	0	1	2	0
F - Fear	2	0	0	1
E - Exercise	0	2	0	1
Column Totals				
Grand total (add up column totals)				

CHOSEN ONE QUIZ RESULTS

Once you have calculated your grand total, find the section below that matches the number of points you got in the quiz. Then read that section to find your results.

Score: 1–8 Points
Great effort! The highest possible score was 28 points.

Your mastery level is that of an Initiate. This means you are not yet aware of the path of the Chosen Ones! You should begin studying and learning. The rewards will be to create liberty, wisdom, and prosperity in your life. Remember the journey towards success begins with a single step. To begin your study, keep reading this book.

Score: 9-13 Points
Good job! The highest possible score was 28 points.

Your mastery level is that of a Novice. This means you have begun the journey but do not yet understand the path of the Chosen Ones and how to proceed! Keep studying and learning as you grow. The reward will be to create liberty, wisdom, and prosperity in your life. Remember the journey towards success begins with a single step. To stay on the path keep reading.

Score: 14-18 Points
Well Done! The highest possible score was 28 points.

Your mastery level is that of an Apprentice. This means your journey has led you to understand many traits of the Chosen Ones! Keep studying and learning as you grow. The reward will be to create liberty, wisdom, and prosperity in your life. Remember the journey towards success begins with a single step. To stay on the path keep reading.

Score: 19-23 Points

Congratulations! The highest possible score was 28 points.

Your mastery level is that of a Journeyman. This means you understand many things and have great potential to become one of the master Chosen Ones! Keep studying, taking action, and learning on this path, and you will create liberty, wisdom, and prosperity in your life. Remember the journey towards success begins with a single step. Stay on the path and keep reading.

Score: 24-28 Points

Amazing! The highest possible score was 28 points.

Your mastery level is that of a Master. This means you have an enlightened understanding and are well on your way to becoming a Self-Chosen One! Keep moving along this path, and you will create much liberty, wisdom, and prosperity in your life. Remember the journey towards success begins with a single step. Action is required to attain this level in real life. To stay on the path keep reading.

~∞~

SPECIAL BONUS!

As a special bonus for reading my book or taking the quiz on my website, you can download a FREE gift. Jim Britt, who is the man who gave Tony Robbins his first job, has recorded some special lessons exclusively for use on *Program Your Life Radio*. Most of the lessons are available for listening on the website, but his lesson on success is reserved for my readers. Go to this URL to download Jim Britt's Lesson on Success.

http://www.programyourlife.org/wp-content/uploads/Jim-Britt-Success-Short-Lesson.mp3

It is my gift to you, and I hope you enjoy it.

If you want to review the most correct answers and scoring for the Chosen One Quiz, please refer to the Appendix in the back of the book. There I break down the questions and explain the points assigned to each answer. I suggest you do this after you have completed reading the entire book. It will make more sense once you have read about the progression of the Chosen Ones.

PART 2

THE PROGRESSION OF THE CHOSEN ONES

8

───※───

INITIATE

THE INITIATE

*The purpose of the initiate level is to become aware,
acknowledge your past and how it affected you.
Then decide that you are capable of much more.*

W elcome to the progression of the chosen ones.
This is where the action and the fun start. In
this part of the book, each chapter will walk
you through the self-chosen one process. You will take on
the role of an initiate, novice, apprentice, journeyman, and
master. Each role has actions and knowledge necessary to
advance to the next level. Some of the concepts are different
ways of thinking, some are choices, and others are tasks to be
performed.

This is your guide to recreating your life, as you've always
wanted it to be. So set some huge goals and don't play small.

Go after your new life with courage and persistence in a way you have never done before. You will love the feeling of really going for it. Are you ready to live a big, expansive life? It is time to start the journey; you will enjoy the ride.

The first chosen one attainment level focuses on awareness of self, others, the world, and acknowledging your present and past circumstances. You start by looking at your past and identifying the experiences that have profoundly affected your life. This will help with overcoming any self-defeating or harmful habits, characteristics, relationships, substances, and define areas for future improvement.

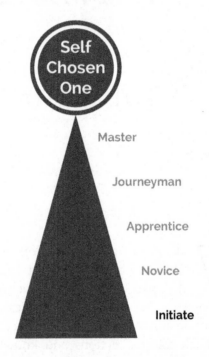

From this new awareness of self, you will create compelling reasons to change as you explore the core beliefs you hold about yourself. You will learn about the power of the subconscious mind, and how it controls our lives. You will begin to understand the importance of giving without having expectations, plus you will be given an awareness of the comfort zone and how it can hold you back. Ultimately, you will commit to a new way of life in order to advance.

Follow the steps in the sections to come, to fully initiate yourself as a self-chosen one. We will start with some key concepts before launching into the real inner work you will want to perform. Once you have completed the steps in this chapter, you will be ready to move forward and become a Novice.

These first steps set the foundation for your future, and if they are not fully completed, you will struggle at the next level. They involve either understanding and accepting a concept or taking an action. Some of the actions you may find difficult, even painful. If so, then they are that much more necessary. Pain must be released before we can move on. It is pain that keeps us stuck.

At each level, we will always start with belief concepts since they are so critically central to personal development, and the core of all self-growth. Then we will end each level chapter with infinite intelligence. This is so we remember we are all connected, and being devoted to a higher purpose is a powerful foundation for our lives.

Understand the Subconscious Mind

Part of expanding your awareness is studying your subconscious mind and the power it possesses. This is because your actions are 95% driven by your subconscious mind. Thus you cannot change your life significantly without it supporting you. Your subconscious mind is similar to a computer that you program to perform routine tasks. For example, learned mental behaviors such as driving or tying a shoe become embedded or programmed in our minds after we master them. After we put these programs into place over time, they can be very hard to dislodge. They also become your mental autopilot; therefore, when you are not actively focused on a task your subconscious mind takes control of your behavior.

Our subconscious programs are put into place when we are young to help us perform repetitive tasks and keep us safe. They are instilled by both reinforcement and emotionally charged events. For example, a scary experience involving an angry dog at a young age could result in a lifelong fear of dogs. Even if we later acknowledge consciously that most dogs are loving animals, a programmed subconscious fear can be very hard to overcome.

The subconscious mind is paramount to growth because it does not easily change. This can cause subconscious actions, thoughts, and emotions to be different from your conscious goals and desires. This is especially true when we decide to make changes in our lives that are a break from our past behavior.

Let's say you decide to become more of a risk taker to meet more friends. When you are consciously thinking about your goal, you can make small changes in your behavior, and you see progress. You can introduce yourself to a stranger, and you have a great conversation. All is good until you refocus your attention on something else, then as your subconscious mind takes over your social behavior reverts to its previous programming.

For example, another opportunity to meet someone presents itself, but you are now thinking about a work problem or your family instead of your goal. Your subconscious mind is in control, and it protects you from strangers as it has always done. You thus avoid this new person and refuse to make eye contact, or you leave the situation. Later you notice what happened and wonder why it is so hard to change.

Let me explain why. Your conscious new desire to meet people has not yet reached your subconscious mind; therefore, your older programmed habits are defeating your efforts to change. Many people often give up at this point, figuring that they are unable to change. The truth is they can change, but to win they need to move their new desires into the subconscious mind.

This is done through repetition of the desired behavior or by imprinting it in the mind through an emotional connection. Using repetition to make a change can take at least 21 days to work. Deeply rooted habits take much longer. It also is possible to create a situation where the new behavior can be associated with a positive emotion. This works much more quickly, and there are personal development courses that focus on this.

At the initiate level, it is not necessary to change your subconscious mind but to be aware of how it affects your behavior. If you are struggling with a new goal, the subconscious mind is probably working against you. This only means that some mental programs need to change, not that you are incapable of changing. Imagine the progress you will make once your subconscious mind is working for you. Your future will be amazing!

Recognize Your Comfort Zone

The comfort zone was mentioned previously. The initiate must understand that comfort can make the journey to becoming a master challenging. As you begin to think about your present and past, you may become uncomfortable, and you may want to quit to remove the discomfort. You must resist this tendency because it is self-sabotage. Don't let the comfort zone steal your dreams.

Progress along the chosen one's path will require doing things that were met with resistance in the past. Different results require different actions and new ways of thinking. Your comfort zone is a very powerful thing. It will fight your efforts to change, and you cannot allow it to win.

Change will require being inconvenienced and taking actions that make you uncomfortable. On the bright side, as you proceed you will find that being comfortable is boring.

A life lived inside the comfort zone quickly becomes bland territory that you have seen before, and actions you have done so many times it hurts. The pain builds the more you stay on this hamster wheel.

You will find that taking risks and being uncomfortable releases the pain. Also, you will achieve far more. If you find yourself stuck in the initiating process, then your comfort zone is probably controlling you.

Growth is never a comfortable process at first but repeatedly breaking through your fear walls will give you the confidence and courage to keep moving forward. Soon you will find that it is exciting to be uncomfortable and what you are capable of doing is only limited by what you believe is possible.

So as you begin to move through the steps that follow, beware of your comfort zone and self-imposed limitations. They will be challenged, and your success relies on your ability to operate in a perturbed and uncomfortable state. Just remember being in a perturbed state of mind greatly increases your intelligence and abilities. That queasy feeling in your chest and stomach is growth in action, so embrace it. It is much more exciting than staying in your comfort zone.

AWARENESS OF SELF

Awareness is an enormous concept of its own. We can be aware of our surroundings and our consciousness. We can be aware of the physical world and that we are alive. We can be aware of our feelings and thoughts. The real question is, what type of awareness will most improve our lives?

We can start by being aware of our past. How did your upbringing affect you? Were your parents or guardians supportive or abusive? Did you develop good self-esteem in your past or a lack of it? Are you fearful of others or trusting? Were you ignored as a child? Did you feel loved? Questions such as these will help you understand how you see the world. Everyone sees the world differently, and your perspective was shaped greatly by your past.

As you consider your past, you may become aware of negative thoughts or beliefs about yourself that have resulted from past experiences. Awareness of how your past has affected you makes it possible for you to consider changing because we cannot change anything of which we are not aware. So familiarize yourself with the past and how it has affected you.

Now let us consider our thoughts. Are you aware that we think tens of thousands of thoughts each day? This is true; however, most of our thoughts are the same ones as the day before. Our thinking has become a pattern or routine with few differences each day. If this is so, then just a few major thoughts are dominating our lives. Would you like to know what they are?

If you take the time to listen to yourself think, you might be surprised at how negative your thinking can be. Do you think in terms of abundance or lack and scarcity? Do you expect bad things to happen? Do you talk kindly to yourself and others? Do you complain to others about problems? Are you critical of others? Do you hold yourself to an impossibly high standard? Listen to yourself and find out.

I had always considered myself a positive person. Inside my head, I was convinced I always looked for the best in life. I even disliked negative people who enjoy complaining. Nevertheless, when I was taking a personal improvement course, a friend began pointing out how many of the things I said were negative or pessimistic. At first, I was annoyed by his comments. This could not be true; I thought he just didn't understand me.

However, his comments gave me the awareness to listen to myself from a new perspective. I started paying attention to what I said which was the same as what I was thinking. It was like a shock to my system! I was saying negative things constantly. I had developed a habit of expecting the worst. Perhaps this was in an attempt not to disappoint myself, but there it was.

Once I became aware of my negative thinking, I began to catch myself when I was in that cycle. When I noticed my mind expecting the worst outcome, I started to interrupt the process and redirect my thinking to positive outcomes. My new awareness gave me the power to change my thinking.

What about your beliefs? Are you aware of your beliefs about yourself and the world? Are you good enough to be a success? Do you matter? Are you afraid to make mistakes? Are you lovable and capable of giving love? Is the world a kind or hostile place? Do you know that your answers to these questions will profoundly affect your approach to life?

Awareness of your beliefs is important because beliefs will lead to certain patterns of thinking. Your thought patterns then will lead to certain actions, inactions, or reactions. Without awareness of beliefs, you are more likely to react to situations and other people. Unless you are aware of your beliefs, you cannot act; you can only react. It is the awareness of the belief that drives our actions and gives us the ability to choose another outcome.

Therefore, when you change your beliefs, you change your actions. This is because your actions will always be consistent with your beliefs. The truth is this: change your beliefs, and you will change your life. This mental linkage cannot be broken.

The next awareness is that of responsibility. Remember; you are responsible for all that you become in this life. Anyone younger than 18 may validly say they are not completely responsible for who they are. However, after that age, everyone can change himself or herself, which makes them responsible for who they have become.

As adults, our past, our thoughts, our beliefs, our habits, and our reactions all become our responsibility. Blame is not a characteristic of chosen ones. It may be difficult to accept this at first, but there is magic in it. Responsibility comes with a cosmic twin known as empowerment. Taking responsibility gives us the power to make changes to improve ourselves as long as we have awareness.

You have more power and potential than you will ever know. What you can accomplish is truly limitless. However, your abilities and skills will always match your beliefs about yourself. So, empower yourself by accepting responsibility for who you have become. Then, vow to do the inner work required to change who you are. Remember; it's an inside job.

Take steps to enhance your awareness, and it will provide you with the information necessary to make any changes you desire. Without self-awareness, we are blind to our shortcomings and unable to control our reactions. There are hands-on awareness courses you can take that can help with this concept. The best one I know is held by PSI Seminars and is called The Basic Seminar. You can find them online at psiseminars.com.

REVIEW PRESENT CIRCUMSTANCES

Are you happy with your current progress in life? Have you expanded your life to achieve your dreams? Or, have you shrunken your dreams to fit into your less than desired life? As an initiate, you get to stop and think about your present situation. Is it what you want or do you have more to give? This evaluation will become the starting point for any future progress.

People who pursue personal development do not lead unsatisfying lives. In fact, they lead good lives and usually achieve a large amount of success. Most have good jobs and loving families. They are thankful for what they have but feel they could be accomplishing much more. They have an inner drive that is still not fulfilled, and they want to be great, not just good.

Let's do a reality check for you. Are your present circumstances not what you ultimately desire? Are you making the money you deserve? Do you have the relationships you want? Is your health as good as it could be? Do you feel good about and love yourself? If you have answered NO to any of these questions, then read on.

I was reluctant at first to explore the possibilities of personal development, as my life was good overall. I had supportive friends, a happy marriage, and family, and a lucrative high-tech job. Other people may have thought I was living the dream. However, in my heart, I was not fulfilled. I realized the good life I had was preventing me from wanting more and from becoming great. Good had become the enemy of great.

My present circumstances masked the fact that I wanted far more success in my life. I wanted my own business, to travel, to control my own time, and to be a creator of ideas, products, and services. I was tired of working for others and making them wealthy, giving away my great ideas, and sick of the slow grind of the corporate world. I wanted out of the rat race and didn't know how.

I had to admit to myself that I wasn't truly happy, had much more to give, and still had a lot to learn. I had to be humble enough to admit that pretending to have a great life was not the same thing as truly living one. I had to overcome my pride and be willing to start again. I had to be willing to expect more for myself and choose a different path. I finally became sick and tired of being sick and tired. Something had to change, and I was finally ready to make improvements.

Are you tired or bored of your current life? Have you been lulled into complacency by a good life but want a great one? If so, then get in touch with those thoughts and feelings. Feel the painful awareness of the unfulfilled life and make a decision to change, then become willing to do whatever it takes to change. Decide never to settle for less again. You are worth it.

∽⌒∽

IDENTIFY BELIEFS ABOUT YOURSELF

Your personal beliefs about what you are capable of doing or accomplishing are paramount. This is because your beliefs create your reality and your feelings. Furthermore, you are capable of doing anything you believe possible for you, and you also are limited by what you believe you are incapable of doing.

If this is true, then why do so many people have such limiting beliefs? Why don't they just change their minds and start living amazing lives? One of the reasons for this problem is that people always want to associate a meaning to everything that happens to them. They believe every event says something about their value as an individual.

For example, when I was very young I wanted to be an entrepreneur. I had many great ideas for products and inventions, and I would tinker in my room building things. At that point, I honestly believed in myself. However, when I shared my ideas with family and friends, they were not supportive. My father had a habit of pointing out flaws in my designs and would bring up questions about marketing and business that I was unable to answer.

Because of this perceived negative feedback, I assigned a meaning to it. I decided that it meant I was not capable of being the inventor I wanted to be. By doing this, I created a limitation in my life that would last for more than 30 years. The reality was that I was always able to figure out everything I needed to be a successful inventor, but my personal beliefs became limited by a negative meaning that I invented.

Once this negative meaning was put in place in my mind, I would spend much of my career working for others instead of myself, believing I was incapable of running the show. The limiting beliefs were of my own invention, but I accepted them as reality. It was not until years later while studying personal development that I learned, I was the only person holding myself back. I alone had the power to change my mind and my beliefs.

What do you believe about yourself? What are you capable of achieving? What do you think you can or cannot do? You create the answer to all these questions by the meaning you have assigned to past events. If negative beliefs exist, consider this, these events could easily have been interpreted in a completely different way.

You have the power to change what they mean in your life by changing your thinking. You can decide, right now, that you are capable of anything, and choose to live a life without limitations. You just have to believe it, and it will be true.

Identify any negative beliefs you have about yourself. Write them down so you are aware of them and can actively work to change them. This process can be emotional, but the results are worth the effort.

Write down below any negative beliefs you hold about yourself. Being aware will allow you to recognize and change them.

1. _____
2. _____
3. _____
4. _____
5. _____

GIVE TO OTHERS WITHOUT EXPECTATIONS

The joy of giving to others cannot be underrated. It feels good to give, and it feels good to receive. Somehow, giving just feels wonderful. It gives us self-esteem and pride. There is nothing like the satisfaction I receive when I see a gift well received, especially if I took time to figure out what that person wanted or needed. The joy and satisfaction are enhanced when I don't expect anything in return.

Giving with an expectation of something in return is not true giving. The expectation of getting something in return bestows an obligation upon the other person. They now have to figure out how to repay the gift. They need to find something of equal value or may be obligated to take some action desired by the giver. This sense of obligation makes the gift something with strings attached.

This is the opposite of giving; it is really taking instead. It is a form of taking by using the gift as a way of obtaining something from the gifted one. I'm sure we have all run into people in the world who operate in this manner. Their gifts come with strings attached. They have expectations that make the gift something we do not enjoy receiving.

True giving does not come with expectations or strings attached. The giver releases any expectations of repayment or retribution. The giver does so simply for the joy received by giving. They do not want recognition for having made the gift. In fact, a great way to practice true giving is to make the gift anonymous. So, the giver will never be known.

A silent satisfaction will be reserved for the giver alone to savor when they need a boost of self-confidence. When a gift cannot be made anonymously, the giver can make clear that the gift must not be repaid. If the receiver wishes to return the favor, ask them to give to another just as you have done.

Paying it forward builds true self-esteem and good will. Make this a habit and your self-worth will truly rise to new heights.

DEFINE AREAS FOR IMPROVEMENT

As an initiate, you start looking for ways to improve yourself and your circumstances. You have just looked at your current life and perhaps decided that it isn't what you desire. So now, you can make a list of what could be better. What isn't working anymore? What would you like to improve?

For me, I was tired of sticking with my technical career and not developing my leadership skills and creativity. I had become a drone that was only focused on tasks and serious subjects. There was little fun in what I was doing in my career. I was also wasting my free time on unproductive games, hobbies and watching too much TV. Negative influences from western media were perverting my attitude, and I had become pessimistic in my outlook.

I wanted to develop a positive mindset and believe that I was capable of anything. Limited beliefs had ruled me for so long and, at first, I was unaware I could change them. I also wanted to improve my relationships with my wife and children, knowing I could give more of myself to my friends and family.

In a personal revelation, I came to understand I was a taker instead of a giver in most of my relationships. I sensed a huge emotional hole in my chest that could not be filled, no matter how much others gave me. That hole was my lack of self-worth. To change, I needed to fill up that hole with so much self-love that I felt like giving instead of taking. I needed to love and accept myself truly, and no one else could do that for me. It was an inside job.

I also wanted more prosperity and excitement in life. I didn't want to spend 40 years working and retire with a modest pension and live in poverty. I wanted the financial means to live anywhere in the world, to travel for fun, and to be with loved ones. I also wanted to teach others what I had discovered, as giving back to society became important to me.

Therefore, I made a list of the things I wanted and the relationships I wanted to improve. The list was designed to take perceived weaknesses and reframe them as strengths. I wrote the list as if it already existed.

I am a successful business owner. I am decisive.

I am capable of obtaining my dreams.

I am a chosen one.

I have an excellent relationship with my wife and family.

I exercise every day.

I enjoy eating healthy food.

I posted this list on my bathroom mirror so I could read it every morning. When reading the words, I get in touch with the feeling of already having accomplished the list. Have you written your list yet? If not, it is time to do it.

Use the space below and identify some areas you want to improve. Write them in a positive way.

1. _____

2. _____

3. _____

4. _____

5. _____

COMMIT TO A NEW WAY OF LIFE

The most important step for the initiate is commitment. This is the difference between success and failure. If you can commit to a new way of living and keep that commitment for the rest of your life, your success is guaranteed. Commitment is not a temporary state.

To illustrate this, let me tell you a story. I, too, have struggled with commitment. For most of my life, I was afraid to commit time to my dreams. I was afraid that I would fail or that it was not the correct goal for me. My commitment was only temporary until something that looked better came along; all of which resulted in a lack of progress in any direction.

It was not until I challenged myself to participate in a 90-day goal setting program that I learned true commitment. In this program, I set four scary goals for myself, then with the support of my coach and team went after those goals with the kind of bold action they deserved.

For me, this process was very intimidating, as I had never before committed to anything for that duration. At times, I woke up at night in a cold sweat and questioned if I really wanted to achieve the goals, however, my coach and team would not allow me to quit. I had to update my coach on my progress every two days, and she would not allow me to give less than my best.

During the 90 days, I created a business and a new form of positive radio media. I met well-known people and achieved things I had only dreamed were possible. As I reached each new goal, I learned how much more I was capable of, and as I became comfortable with being uncomfortable, I learned what true commitment meant.

This is the type of commitment you must be willing to make to change your life. You must make a decision that has no chicken exits due to fear or timeframes for failure. You must be willing to keep going *until* you are successful *until* you are healthy *until* you have the relationships desired. When you can make that kind of commitment, then you are ready to advance to novice.

Remember, there are no incorrect goals or dreams. You cannot make a mistake. Anything you can commit to will lead to a better place. It is the process of commitment that we must learn to become a master. All the other lessons in this book are useless without commitment. Can you do it?

If so, then take the top item from your areas for improvement list and make a new statement. Write it out in large letters on a separate sheet of paper or below. Start with "I commit to..." and then write your goal to change. This statement does not need a deadline, as you will keep going until it is achieved. Even it takes a lifetime of work.

I commit to _____

_____

_____

If this statement gives you a strong emotion of elation, hope, or even fear, then it is a good statement. Take some time to feel that emotion because it will provide the energy you need to achieve it. If it does not touch you inside, then make a new one that does. Unless you have compelling dreams and goals to which you can commit, you are not ready to advance to novice.

Take your statement and post it where you can see it every day, then practice feeling a sense of commitment when you read it. When you know you will not give up on this; you are ready to advance to novice. As a novice, you will rediscover how special you are by learning to accept and forgive yourself.

AWARENESS OF THE UNIVERSE

Your awareness of the laws of the universe is critical to the journey upon which we must all embark. Consider this: we live on a planet that is traveling at 67,000 mph around the sun. Our Earth is spinning at 1,000 mph at the equator, and yet we feel no movement. Our sun is a burning star with enough gravity to hold the earth and all the other planets in our solar system in orbit around it.

As vast as our solar system is, it is only one of more than a billion that make up our galaxy. Beyond that, there are at least 125 billion other galaxies in our universe. Yet, our planet is the only one we know of that contains the right conditions for human life.

There is much more about our world and galaxy that we don't understand than we do, including that our lives and interrelationships are bigger than we're aware. Everything we think we know about life is probably incorrect, just as we used to think the earth was flat. There appears to be a grand design to the universe that defies our understanding. Science proves this.

Given the amazing universe, we must know our existence has meaning and cannot be a random event. We are part of a vast cosmic process that is infinitely interrelated and fragile. In fact, quantum physics has taught us that our minds are incredibly powerful. We can change the world around us just by using our minds. Science is in awe of this power, and we can use it to alter reality.

Our thoughts can literally change our lives. If we think negative thoughts, then our lives become a series of unhappy events. If however, we think positive thoughts, our lives will begin to transform to happy events and outcomes. Anything that we think about all the time will come into our lives. As Mike Dooley says, "thoughts become things."

Begin to be aware of your thoughts. Do you expect a positive or negative outcome in any situation? Do you routinely complain to others about your life, the economy, politics, or any topic you choose? Your words speak more loudly than your thoughts. Listen to what you say to determine your true, inner mental state.

Do you blame others for your situation or past events? In the past, other people such as your parents and teachers had a huge effect on your life. Become aware of how others have influenced your thoughts and opinions.

In fact, most of your opinions in life have probably come from others. You probably adopted them. Are you ready to take responsibility for your life and opinions? Do you have the strength to be different from others?

Become aware that you do not need to be a product of your environment. Regardless of how or where you were raised, now as an adult, you can choose to be anything you want to be. You have tremendous power to change your situation and circumstances. You have total control over your mind and how you think. When you are aware of your true power, anything you desire is obtainable.

As an initiate, you must expand your awareness of your true potential and the amazing world in which you live. You must rediscover a sense of wonder about the world and begin to imagine a life without limits. You must expand your consciousness to understand that you already have everything you need within. There is nothing externally that can make you whole.

There is also a force in the universe that is far greater than we are. We must learn to work with it and harness its power. When we work in harmony with the universe, anything is possible. When we work against it, our lives become fearful, small, and difficult. There is a vast universal power of love and creativity that wants to connect with you.

Some of you may already have established a connection with a higher power. If so, then you are already in alignment with infinite intelligence. As we go up the chosen one levels, this connection will be further expanded.

THE MYTH THAT BEING MEDIOCRE IS OKAY

In movies and television today, it's popular and celebrated to be mediocre. Many shows portray people living with dead-end jobs, messed up family lives, and even addictions. In watching these shows you get the idea that this is the way life is supposed to be, so just settle in.

The characters have lost all hope of a better life and have become sarcastic about it. They are stuck in a rut of family drama, bad luck, and may be using some form of self-defeating behavior to cope with it. They overeat, shop, exercise, play games, watch TV, or have sex in excess. We see this so often now that being stuck in addiction has become normal. Unfortunately, this leads people to feel like victims of circumstances.

The message seems to be that it is okay to be this way. It's okay to be an alcoholic, underachiever, sex addict, or obese. It's okay to have a crappy job, to live in a bad relationship, or to have screwed up kids. Why should you change your life if you see it as acceptable on TV?

The problem with such standards is they set the bar too low for your life. I know it feels good to see someone else struggling with their life. In fact, many people shown in the media are far more messed up than the average westerner. We can find solace in seeing others more messed up than we are, as it makes us feel good about ourselves.

I do think it is great to feel good about yourself. I'm all for it. I think we should feel good as much as possible. However, I suggest we feel good for legitimate reasons. Let's feel good because we did well in school, found a great job, or met someone special. Let's feel good because we became a responsible parent or did a good deed. Let's feel good for overcoming obstacles.

If your life is not where you want it to be, then you will naturally not feel good. Use this as valuable feedback that change is required, then concentrate on improvement. If we fill our lives with feeling good about falsehoods, then we are living a lie. I believe we need to have a higher standard for our lives than we see in the media. We want to be working to improve our relationships. We want to be trying harder in school. We want to be moving up in our careers or starting our own businesses. We need not rob ourselves of valuable feedback.

I'm not saying that we should feel bad all the time. Everyone needs to have fun in life and wants freedom from their worries. However, there are many ways to do this without lowering our standards.

If we lower our standards far enough, we will feel better about our mediocre lives, and we can compare ourselves to others who are less fortunate. We can tell ourselves, at least I can pay my bills, and at least I'm not as bad as that guy in the movie. That may work for a while, maybe even for a lifetime. If we do this and accept being mediocre, we may even feel happy about life, but it won't be a fulfilled life. The problem is, being mediocre doesn't leave enough room to have dreams.

In order to have dreams, you need to be better than average. Dreams require a higher standard, one that modern culture rarely shows us. Dreams require that we evaluate where we are and become dissatisfied. Only by becoming dissatisfied, can we take ourselves to a higher level. Yes, we will feel unhappy for a while, but that unhappiness becomes a reason for moving forward, a reason for changing our lives, a reason to fix that relationship, and a reason to quit that job. It provides us a reason to start a business, a reason to seek help for compulsive behaviors if necessary, and a reason for expecting more from ourselves.

People with dreams and vision have the stuff of greatness. Men and women of great accomplishment and wealth all have dreams, and those without dreams will end up working for those who do. Read the biography of any person of accomplishment, and you'll see that their dreams drove them. It got them out of bed early every morning and kept them up at night. They taught themselves what was necessary, or sought out assistance from others. They molded themselves into a person who could achieve their dreams and forgot about their worries, feelings of inadequacy, and shortcomings. They concentrated on strengths instead of weaknesses.

So the falsehood that mediocrity is okay must be replaced by the truth that we must live to a higher standard. We have a need to dream, to allow those dreams to consume us, and to mold our lives into what is necessary to accomplish them. The dreams themselves are important. We will celebrate their accomplishment and reap the rewards when finished. However, it is who we will become along the way that is most important. We will become a person who is confident, capable, and inspired. Become a leader who can overcome large obstacles and, more importantly, overcome themselves.

The truth is we all are extraordinary. We all won the genetic lottery and were born into this fantastic world. That itself is an amazing accomplishment. Now, let's go on and live an amazing life that is worthy of who we really are.

CHAPTER SUMMARY

The benefits of moving through the self-chosen one initiate process cannot be underestimated. As you do this, you will discover more about yourself than you ever have before. You will know you are ready to advance to a novice when you have a desire for a better life, identified limiting beliefs, defined areas for improvement, and committed to overcome them as never before. You can do it, and the rewards will be unbelievable.

This was a difficult step for me. I had studied personal development concepts in the past. Learning them on an intellectual level was helpful, but it did not lead to change. I had attempted to overcome my limiting beliefs by learning new skills and strategies but was not connecting on an emotional level.

I was convinced that all I needed was a better business strategy, so I attended real estate and stock marketing courses. The result was always the same. I would get only so far and then quit. I always hit a mental or emotional wall. I finally discovered what I needed was not new strategies but to overturn my limited beliefs. I needed to make the journey from my head to my heart.

In my heart, I still didn't fully believe I deserved to be successful and happy. The improvement needed was inside of me instead of outside as I had always assumed. Now, all the failures made sense, and I knew what to do. The next step was to commit to overcoming my false beliefs.

This required more commitment than I had ever employed before. I committed to leaving my past behind and live in the faith of my greatness in the future. I committed to a life of personal development, not just a few books and courses. I committed to doing whatever it took change myself because

I didn't want to live the old way anymore. This commitment I still keep today.

As a review, the steps an initiate will go through are listed below.

1. Understand the subconscious mind
2. Recognize your comfort zone
3. Awareness of self
4. Review present circumstances
5. Identify beliefs about yourself
6. Give to others without expectations
7. Commit to a new way of life
8. Define areas for improvement
9. Become aware of the universe
10. Lose the myth that being mediocre is okay

9

~~~

NOVICE

THE NOVICE

*The purpose of the novice level is to choose yourself
and accept your greatness. Accept all your flaws
and forgive any past mistakes or failures.*

Welcome to the second attainment level of the chosen ones. Here you will leave your past behind. You will learn to stop living in the past or future and return to living in the present as you did as a child. You will make a bold decision to choose yourself for greatness. You will take responsibility for your place in life. You will begin to forgive yourself and others. As a benefit, you will stop being hard on yourself.

You will cast off the expectations of others and live for yourself and what you want. You will stop making up stories about what other people think of you. You will also choose your values, evaluate your health and realize the high price you may have paid for being normal.

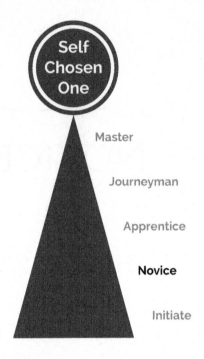

Your future is bright, as you have found the path and a guide through the maze of the self-development journey. Don't worry about the destination yet. You just have to keep taking the next step. Trust the process, and you will emerge as a master of yourself and the world. Let us begin again with a topic on belief.

CHOOSE YOURSELF FOR GREATNESS

The first step as a novice on the path of the chosen ones is to recognize that no one is born of greatness. No one has a destiny that was ordained by a higher power. Regardless of what Hollywood or books would have you believe, greatness is a decision, not a destiny or calling.

The people who are having success made a choice that most do not. They chose themselves for greatness. They did not wait for others to choose them and they did not worry about whether they had any innate skills or advantages. They just developed themselves into whatever was necessary to succeed.

This is the true story that the world does not want you to know. If you, the average person, could only realize your true potential, the top 5% of the world would quiver in their fancy slippers. They know they cannot control large amounts of wealth in a world where people understand their value.

If you have not made the decision to choose yourself for greatness yet, it should happen now as a novice. You already have everything required to obtain your dreams. Also, you can develop any skill, and learn any desired knowledge along the way.

Believing in yourself begins with the simple act of choosing yourself for greatness. You will no longer settle for mediocrity in life. You think of yourself as a superstar. When writing a movie or play about the world, you will give yourself a leading role. You surround yourself with other superstars. You no longer hang out with people you do not think highly of, or who do not think highly of you.

You treat yourself and life seriously but still have lots of fun. You feel important and acknowledge the skills and abilities that you possess. You are humble but don't downplay your worth. When someone gives you a compliment you accept it and say, "Thank you."

Choosing yourself for greatness is not a selfish act. You are simply affirming your place in the universe and the magnificence it wants for you. When we do not choose ourselves for greatness, we deny the will of the universe. It wants only the best for you and from you. When you choose yourself, you are placing yourself on the path that the divine created for you to follow.

So make your commitment now to choose yourself for greatness. You deserve as much as anyone because we are all equals. You can't afford to wait any longer; write yourself a starring role in your own life. This is your new beginning—do it now.

I am one of the chosen ones! I don't need anyone else to choose me. I am extraordinary, and I matter. I can change the world. I choose myself for greatness! I will wait no longer!

FORGIVE YOURSELF

Astonishingly, forgiveness is one of the secret keys to personal development. This is because past events and judgments can keep us stuck unless we let go of them. We cannot fully embrace the future while we are still holding onto the past. This is especially true for understanding how we sometimes mistreat ourselves.

Forgiveness comes in two forms: forgiveness of self and others. When we hold grudges and judgments against others, we also hold them against ourselves. In fact, whenever we judge another we are also judging ourselves by the same standard. Unforgivable actions of others become our unforgivable actions because no one is perfect, and we all make mistakes.

These judgments and grudges that we hold against others become applied to us, and this then manifests in self-loathing, and self-sabotage. We can ultimately hold ourselves in contempt, resulting in habits and thoughts which are self-defeating. Our subconscious mind understands this contempt and makes sure our positive actions are prevented from success.

We can only overcome this self-loathing by forgiving ourselves and withholding judgments. Ironically, according to Walter Jacobson, this cannot be accomplished directly. In his book *Forgive to Win,* Jacobson states that we can only forgive ourselves by forgiving others first, and by performing esteem-able acts.

By forgiving others and developing nonjudgmental thoughts about others, we become forgivable in our minds. Once we stop judging others, we stop judging ourselves. Once we forgive others, we begin to forgive ourselves. Once we forgive ourselves, we stop sabotaging our thoughts and actions. Wouldn't you love to stop sabotaging yourself?

Do you hold grudges and judge others harshly? If so, then this behavior will result in your own self-loathing and self-sabotage. The finger pointed at another always points back to us as well. Instead, become a forgiving person who does not complain about the actions of others. You will ultimately feel better about yourself, which will allow you to move forward in life without feeling unworthy.

TAKE RESPONSIBILITY

As an initiate, you were able to look at your past to figure out the influences that affected your life. When you were young, you had little control over your environment and could blame others for the outcomes. Now as a novice, you must forget the past and take responsibility for everything in your life. Regardless of past circumstances, your life belongs to you now, and only you can change it.

The novice begins to live from the place of personal responsibility. Don't seek to justify, blame, or shame when things go wrong because those actions create no value. If you do not grow from the experience of making mistakes, you will be doomed to repeat the same mistakes over again. This is why many people make very little progress towards their goals. They are not learning along the way because they blame others instead of learning the lesson.

When you take responsibility for your actions, you are essentially asking, "What can I learn from this?" Every mistake or tough situation contains a lesson. The choices to justify, blame, and shame contain no opportunity for learning. According to Marshall Thurber, you must become a constant learner.

By taking responsibility for who we are, we take back the control of our life and future. It relieves stress to admit that we don't know everything, and we are still learning as we go. We can release the perfectionism that keeps us from admitting our mistakes and apply the life lessons gained from mistakes so that our outcomes improve.

Choose Your Values

As you will discover, personal values are the foundation upon which a fulfilled life is always built. The novice who has chosen their values and explicitly written them down can use them at the next level as an apprentice, to create their life as they have always desired.

Your personal values and vices exercise control over your life whether you know it or not. They may be unconscious, and you may not even be able to name them. However, your actions reveal them to the world, and they affect every decision or thought you have.

Values that are positive and inspiring will lead to a happy and successful life. Vices are less productive and may lead to unhappiness. That's why it's important to actually identify or choose your values and reduce your vices to progress. The process of making conscious choices about them is critical since they so directly influence behavior.

If you are not comprehensive in this process, you may mistake a vice for a virtue or have no guiding principles to use as your yardstick in making decisions. Everyone has experienced times when they needed to make a tough decision where two choices seemed equal. Values are the tiebreaker, and they make the choices much easier.

Some people believe they must find themselves, and that by exploring the world they will realize their true nature and calling. I am not a fan of this theory. I believe that you create yourself. Your destiny is of your own design and not predestined by anyone or anything. Your destiny starts with your values. You choose the ones that are most important to you and then it sets your course in the world. All the other steps in creating yourself are based on these values. Once chosen, use them as a guide throughout the rest of the process of creation.

My personal values include honesty, integrity, responsibility, respect, and persistence. I suggest you choose your own and place them somewhere they can always be visible. Once you do, they become your criteria for decisions in your life. So when faced with a choice, and you are having a tough time choosing, always go to your values. Which decision is most in alignment with your values? This is the best way forward.

Another guide is to consider which decision will make you feel better about yourself. This will not always be the easiest path, but any choice that makes you feel better about yourself is a good one. In the end, happiness, which leads to success is all about how we feel about ourselves.

So let's go through the process of choosing your values. If you have done this before, simply choose them again and reconfirm in your mind how important they are to you. Below is a list of values you can use to begin. This is a complete list, and it will help provide ideas if this exercise is unfamiliar. Review the list below, choose your top five values and then circle them. Once you have done that, write them in the blanks in order of your priorities. This way your most important value will be listed first and then your second.

Take a few minutes to think about what's important to you. It could be family, love, appreciation, honesty, integrity, etc. I have always believed that responsibility and integrity should be on everyone's list, however, choose your own. It is your life, and you are the master. It's time to choose. Please don't skip this step, it is critical to your future success.

1. Abundance	34. Attractiveness	67. Closeness
2. Acceptance	35. Audacity	68. Comfort
3. Accessibility	36. Availability	69. Commitment
4. Accomplishment	37. Awareness	70. Community
5. Accountability	38. Awe	71. Compassion
6. Accuracy	39. Balance	72. Competence
7. Achievement	40. Beauty	73. Competition
8. Acknowledgment	41. Being the best	74. Completion
9. Activeness	42. Belonging	75. Composure
10. Adaptability	43. Benevolence	76. Concentration
11. Adoration	44. Bliss	77. Confidence
12. Adroitness	45. Boldness	78. Conformity
13. Advancement	46. Bravery	79. Congruency
14. Adventure	47. Brilliance	80. Connection
15. Affection	48. Buoyancy	81. Consciousness
16. Affluence	49. Calmness	82. Conservation
17. Aggressiveness	50. Camaraderie	83. Consistency
18. Agility	51. Candor	84. Contentment
19. Alertness	52. Capability	85. Continuity
20. Altruism	53. Care	86. Contribution
21. Amazement	54. Carefulness	87. Control
22. Ambition	55. Celebrity	88. Conviction
23. Amusement	56. Certainty	89. Conviviality
24. Anticipation	57. Challenge	90. Coolness
25. Appreciation	58. Change	91. Cooperation
26. Approachability	59. Charity	92. Cordiality
27. Approval	60. Charm	93. Correctness
28. Art	61. Chastity	94. Country
29. Articulacy	62. Cheerfulness	95. Courage
30. Artistry	63. Clarity	96. Courtesy
31. Assertiveness	64. Cleanliness	97. Craftiness
32. Assurance	65. Clear-minded	98. Creativity
33. Attentiveness	66. Cleverness	99. Credibility

100. Cunning	132. Effectiveness	164. Fearlessness
101. Curiosity	133. Efficiency	165. Ferocity
102. Daring	134. Elation	166. Fidelity
103. Decisiveness	135. Elegance	167. Fierceness
104. Decorum	136. Empathy	168. Financial independence
105. Deference	137. Encouragement	169. Firmness
106. Delight	138. Endurance	170. Fitness
107. Dependability	139. Energy	171. Flexibility
108. Depth	140. Enjoyment	172. Flow
109. Desire	141. Entertainment	173. Fluency
110. Determination	142. Enthusiasm	174. Focus
111. Devotion	143. Environmentalism	175. Fortitude
112. Devoutness	144. Ethics	176. Frankness
113. Dexterity	145. Euphoria	177. Freedom
114. Dignity	146. Excellence	178. Friendliness
115. Diligence	147. Excitement	179. Friendship
116. Direction	148. Exhilaration	180. Frugality
117. Directness	149. Expectancy	181. Fun
118. Discipline	150. Expediency	182. Gallantry
119. Discovery	151. Experience	183. Generosity
120. Discretion	152. Expertise	184. Gentility
121. Diversity	153. Exploration	185. Giving
122. Dominance	154. Expressiveness	186. Grace
123. Dreaming	155. Extravagance	187. Gratitude
124. Drive	156. Extroversion	188. Gregariousness
125. Duty	157. Exuberance	189. Growth
126. Dynamism	158. Fairness	190. Guidance
127. Eagerness	159. Faith	191. Happiness
128. Ease	160. Fame	192. Harmony
129. Economy	161. Family	193. Health
130. Ecstasy	162. Fascination	194. Heart
131. Education	163. Fashion	195. Helpfulness

196. Heroism	229. Joy	262. Obedience
197. Holiness	230. Judiciousness	263. Open-mindedness
198. Honesty	231. Justice	264. Openness
199. Honor	232. Keenness	265. Optimism
200. Hopefulness	233. Kindness	266. Order
201. Hospitality	234. Knowledge	267. Organization
202. Humility	235. Leadership	268. Originality
203. Humor	236. Learning	269. Outdoors
204. Hygiene	237. Liberation	270. Outlandishness
205. Imagination	238. Liberty	271. Outrageousness
206. Impact	239. Lightness	272. Partnership
207. Impartiality	240. Liveliness	273. Patience
208. Independence	241. Logic	274. Passion
209. Individuality	242. Longevity	275. Peace
210. Industry	243. Love	276. Perceptiveness
211. Influence	244. Loyalty	277. Perfection
212. Ingenuity	245. Majesty	278. Perkiness
213. Inquisitiveness	246. Making a difference	279. Perseverance
214. Insightfulness	247. Marriage	280. Persistence
215. Inspiration	248. Mastery	281. Persuasiveness
216. Integrity	249. Maturity	282. Philanthropy
217. Intellect	250. Meaning	283. Piety
218. Intelligence	251. Meekness	284. Playfulness
219. Intensity	252. Mellowness	285. Pleasantness
220. Intimacy	253. Meticulousness	286. Pleasure
221. Intrepidness	254. Mindfulness	287. Poise
222. Introspection	255. Modesty	288. Polish
223. Introversion	256. Motivation	289. Popularity
224. Intuition	257. Mysteriousness	290. Potency
225. Intuitiveness	258. Nature	291. Power
226. Inventiveness	259. Neatness	292. Practicality
227. Investing	260. Nerve	293. Pragmatism
228. Involvement	261. Nonconformity	294. Precision

295. Preparedness	328. Rigor	361. Spirituality
296. Presence	329. Sacredness	362. Spontaneity
297. Pride	330. Sacrifice	363. Spunk
298. Privacy	331. Sagacity	364. Stability
299. Proactivity	332. Saintliness	365. Status
300. Professionalism	333. Sanguinity	366. Stealth
301. Prosperity	334. Satisfaction	367. Stillness
302. Prudence	335. Science	368. Strength
303. Punctuality	336. Security	369. Structure
304. Purity	337. Self-control	370. Success
305. Rationality	338. Selflessness	371. Support
306. Realism	339. Self-reliance	372. Supremacy
307. Reason	340. Self-respect	373. Surprise
308. Reasonableness	341. Sensitivity	374. Sympathy
309. Recognition	342. Sensuality	375. Synergy
310. Recreation	343. Serenity	376. Teaching
311. Refinement	344. Service	377. Teamwork
312. Reflection	345. Sexiness	378. Temperance
313. Relaxation	346. Sexuality	379. Thankfulness
314. Reliability	347. Sharing	380. Thoroughness
315. Relief	348. Shrewdness	381. Thoughtfulness
316. Religiousness	349. Significance	382. Thrift
317. Reputation	350. Silence	383. Tidiness
318. Resilience	351. Silliness	384. Timeliness
319. Resolution	352. Simplicity	385. Traditionalism
320. Resolve	353. Sincerity	386. Tranquility
321. Resourcefulness	354. Skillfulness	387. Transcendence
322. Respect	355. Solidarity	388. Trust
323. Responsibility	356. Solitude	389. Trustworthiness
324. Rest	357. Sophistication	390. Truth
325. Restraint	358. Soundness	391. Understanding
326. Reverence	359. Speed	392. Unflappability
327. Richness	360. Spirit	393. Uniqueness

394. Unity	403. Vitality	412. Winning
395. Usefulness	404. Vivacity	413. Wisdom
396. Utility	405. Volunteering	414. Wittiness
397. Valor	406. Warmhearted	415. Wonder
398. Variety	407. Warmth	416. Worthiness
399. Victory	408. Watchfulness	417. Youthfulness
400. Vigor	409. Wealth	418. Zeal
401. Virtue	410. Willfulness	
402. Vision	411. Willingness	

Write your top five values in order of priority below:

1. _____
2. _____
3. _____
4. _____
5. _____

By choosing your top five values, you have now completed a critical development task that most people have never done. This simple act of identifying and writing them down in order will plant them into your mind and help you resolve critical decisions. It will also affect your behavior as you will automatically begin to create things in alignment with these values in your life.

Take your list above, write it on a piece of paper, and post it on your bathroom mirror. Read them every day as you prepare to go out into the world. Ideas on how to bring them into your life will spring forth.

One of the reasons that choosing your values is so important is because an enlightened life is about being committed to something bigger than you are. Values are ideas that are eternal, although we can become one with them. We can serve these ideals. We can take them as our own and become a mechanism to implement them in the world.

Suppose you chose creativity as your top value. You will soon discover everything you do begins to reflect this. You may decide to become a painter, sculptor, or actor. Your objective then becomes to be excellent at being creative.

Your previous focus may have been to make some money selling your drawings. However, now money is no longer the focus of the goal. Your path to an enlightened life is to foster creativity in yourself and others. This may lead indirectly to wealth, but your goal of being supremely creative is much bigger than your need for money. Just as many of us are motivated to serve others, we also are motivated to work for an idea greater than ourselves.

Suppose you chose world peace as your top value. Now you begin to bring it into your life. You don't need to be elected to Congress or become a foreign missionary to bring this about. You can start in your neighborhood or your home. Bring peace within yourself first. Make peace with your past and your unrealistic expectations for yourself. Forgive yourself and others for any offenses.

Then bring peace within your family. Restore strained relationships. Forgive your siblings, children, and parents. Refuse to bring up the past and live in the now. Make amends to your spouse if necessary. Begin to see their good qualities and ignore their shortcomings. Rediscover the things that brought you together. Come from love and peace in everything you do.

Bring peace to your neighborhood. Get to know your neighbors. Look out for their interests as well as your own. Respect other people's property and personal space. If you live in close quarters, be aware of how your actions affect others. Greet the benefits that diversity brings. You can learn much more from people that are not like you than you can from those that look and act like you.

Bring peace in your state or country. Support those leaders that speak of tolerance, change, and love. Reject those that stall progress and vilify people and organizations. People who project hate and refer to others as "them and us" are not for peace. Peace comes from love and acceptance. Support any organization that is committed to higher values.

Once committed to something bigger than ourselves we are no longer in ego. We can enroll others in our cause. We tap into the power of the universe that wants to bring more of this into the world. We can then set the vision for our lives. Setting a vision allows us to access all the power of our conscious and subconscious mind.

Having a vision for your life is one of the necessary stepping stones to becoming one of the chosen ones. If you have not already done so, set a goal now to create a vision for your life. Once you do this, everything will begin to come into alignment within your life. You will have created your purpose and have new, unlimited energy to obtain it. You will begin to behave automatically in a way consistent with your vision. Decisions that previously stumped you will become easy and obvious.

REMOVE NEGATIVE INFLUENCES

Our environment can control us if we don't actively manage it. There can be so much trash in our environments that we are unable to focus. I'm talking about the garbage that can fill our minds with minutiae and absorb our precious time. We must win the war for our own attention against the advertisers and distractors and instead, focus our time where it will sow fertile seeds to grow our new future.

Winning the war for your attention includes removing the distractions and unproductive habits that keep you busy doing non-important things. Most people are very busy doing things that do not add value. For many, the top of this list is their daily habit of watching TV. TV can be informative and a great outlet when we need to unwind, but it easily can expand to absorb all your time and attention.

Watching sports is very enjoyable for many. For example, I love to watch NFL football. This means that for several months a year, my Sunday, Monday, and Thursday evenings can be completely devoted to watching games. Fortunately for me, NFL football is the only sport I watch, but many also watch Baseball, Soccer, and Basketball, so the process keeps going year round.

There is a lot of enjoyment that comes from watching sports on TV, but it comes with an opportunity cost—your time. You cannot get your time back, and plenty of focused time is required to create an exciting life. Spending less time on leisure pursuits is the price that must be paid for a better life, and what many don't know is that time we spend working on our goals is fun, too.

As an example of a negative influence, consider the nightly TV news. Most of the newscast is devoted to covering negative stories. There is always a crisis story to be told somewhere in the world, and they will go anywhere to find it. The price of keeping up with the world is being exposed to the constant flow of negative news. I like to be informed too, but hearing about tragedies every day won't change the world, and it becomes depressing.

How do you feel after watching the news? You may be keeping up on current events but becoming cynical in your mind every time you do it. You end up feeling rotten. The reports are increasing the evil in the world by spreading it into our homes every night. Get your news elsewhere where you can pick the topics you follow. Then, look for what's good in the world instead.

Do you spend lots of time on the Internet in your free time? There are a million ways to kill time online. Social networks such as Facebook, Twitter, and YouTube have grabbed the attention of both young and old. The feed of trivial "news" that comes from these networks is slightly amusing but consumes thousands of hours each year.

The influence of these networks is mostly negative as well. They are full of advertising, sad stories, pictures of food, complainers, and retreads of the same old videos. A rare post is actually worth your time. Unless you are using social networks as a business, you should not be spending much time there. You need your time for more productive endeavors.

Video games are the biggest time killer of them all. Gamers, as they are called, can spend the equivalent of years online. Thousands of hours and dollars are wasted even if you are a casual gamer. Being an avid gamer will almost guarantee you a mediocre life due to time lost. You have to focus your attention on your real life, not your virtual life, to succeed.

The depiction of violence, crime, and degradation in games is another reason to avoid them. The characters in many of these games are hardly role models. It might be fun but everything you do, even online, matters. Pretending to be evil in a video game has real-world effects on your mind.

Unless you are a video game developer, stay away from video games, especially the violent ones. They can absorb your future.

Another time waster is texting whether via cell phone or an online chat client. This includes photo messaging apps such as Snapchat. Chat is a great way to keep up to date with people and is more efficient than voice for short communications. However, it is not good if you find yourself sending hundreds of messages or pictures per day. Constant communications can absorb time and energy which you may not have to spare. Besides, we have all seen too many selfies.

The last area of potential negative influences is negative people and relationships. Everyone knows someone who only wants to complain. They always want to talk about what's wrong with the world, how unfair things are, how corrupt companies and the government are, and the latest horrible story on the news. They have a negative view of the world and want everyone else to know about it.

Do you know someone who does this? Do you do this? If so, then either change your mindset or find new friends and relationships. This way of thinking will keep you stuck in your current situation. These people despise those that are happy. They want to pull everyone down to their level. Anyone who desires a better life is a threat to them.

You must avoid negative people and negative mindsets. It is poison for the chosen ones. So many positive people will help you along the way. You just need to start spending time with them instead of those that are stuck and are not willing to do anything about it. You cannot change other people; they must want it for themselves.

HEALTH EVALUATION

Our health is our most prized possession. To keep ourselves healthy and feeling good we must pay attention to how we treat our bodies. This includes the amount of exercise we get, stretching, muscle mass, and range of motion, as well as our eating habits. If you haven't thought about your health for a while, this is a good time to review and consider areas for improvement.

Technology has made the world a sedentary place for many people. Machines take care of many of our chores. Unfortunately, this lack of activity can lead to a variety of health issues such as weight gain, loss of muscle mass, diabetes, and poor nutrition. Serious injuries can occur when your body is not kept fit. You could even tear your ACL just by getting up from the couch if your joints are weak from neglect.

Consider your physical body and decide whether you are happy with your fitness. Are you carrying extra weight or lacking stamina? Are you less than satisfied when you look in the mirror? What about your range of motion? Is your body as flexible as you want it to be? If not, then adding this to your goals list is a good idea. You will create your goals list at the next level as an apprentice. Below, jot down some health areas you would like to improve:

1. _____

2. _____

3. _____

What you eat has a dramatic effect on your health. Although it is one of the most critical areas you can change to improve how you feel, most doctors do not provide nutrition advice. Instead, they offer drugs to counteract the effects of poor eating and exercise habits. Drugs do not solve the problem, they just alleviate the symptoms until your body begins to breakdown from the ill health.

Our bodies were not designed to consume vast amounts of carbohydrates, sugar, and meat. Unfortunately, many people eat poorly because of the foods offered by fast food and other typical restaurants. These products are also heavily advertised because they are very profitable for the manufacturers. It can be more difficult and expensive to find and eat fruits, lean meats, and vegetables.

To become a master chosen one, you will need enough physical energy to move through the levels and create your dreams. You will want to optimize your health so tasks will take less time, and you will not run out of gas along the road ahead. So take care of your body through better exercise and nutrition. You deserve it.

DON'T MAKE UP STORIES

One of the more remarkable tricks our mind can play on us is story making. Even simple life events can trigger our mind to go into story making mode where we decide in advance how a future event or conversation will go, or even what another person is thinking. This habit can be unhelpful and is usually an incorrect version of what is or what will be. We are not mind readers or sages of the future, so do not be deluded.

The problem with story making is that stories we make up are often negative, which lead us to believe the outcomes will be undesirable. Then, based on the negative story we just made up, we change our behavior to avoid this fictitious situation. Thus, the fake story we made up can stop us from moving towards our goals. What could be more self-defeating than this?

The truth is that we do not know what others are thinking about us or anything else. Those that believe they do are fooling themselves. You might be correct occasionally, but nobody has this magic power of reading minds. The best course of action is not to make up stories, and not worry about what others are thinking. If you have to imagine something, think of a positive outcome.

To combat negative stories, imagine only the best outcome in every situation such as others like you, they think you are talented, smart, and even brilliant. Also, decide that the future only holds positive events for you such as you will be happy, healthy, and wealthy. Everything you do is turning out fabulous. Use story making to your advantage.

When you do this, you will be encouraged to take actions that move you forward. You will become excited about your future, and good things will happen because you expect them.

When negative thoughts appear, replace them with a positive version of the situation.

Use your mind to imagine your future as you want it to be, and don't waste time thinking about what could go wrong. This process alone can completely change your life. It will help you focus on what you want instead of what you do not want. So use your ability to make up stories for your benefit and eliminate those negative stories, because the future never happens in that way.

Meditation Walking

As an initiate, you became aware of the universe and how it wants the best for you. It is also a conduit to all knowledge and vast creativity. A great way to connect with this infinite intelligence is through the practice of relaxation cycle, also known as meditation. Meditation has been practiced for centuries and from my research is used by many successful people.

The benefits of meditation are numerous. It can be used for relaxation, enhancing creativity, deep thinking, and accessing the super-conscious. You can also create a virtual workshop for use during your meditations. Thomas Edison called his meditation sessions going to his workshop. He accumulated over 2,000 patents using this technique.

When you build a virtual workshop, fantastic results are possible. You can access the skills and abilities of assistants and advisors that you summon upon demand. Meditation is also a way to take time for yourself, relax, and acknowledge your gifts and abilities.

For those people who have not started their meditation practice, a great way to begin is by doing a walking meditation. I use this on a regular basis, so it is not just for beginners. A walking meditation is best done alone. You'll want to be silent during this time you take just for you. I recommend doing this in the morning, so you get to implement the benefits immediately in your day.

The ideal length for a walking meditation is 30-60 minutes; however, 15 minutes is long enough to gain the benefits. The best environment for this is outside, as the feeling of being in nature enhances the benefits. To clear any additional distractions that may arise, make sure you have on comfortable shoes and warm clothing.

Begin your walking meditation by taking some deep breaths to clear any stress or anxiety that has built up during the day. Then walk at a comfortable pace and begin to remove any thoughts that are troubling you. Within the first five minutes of walking, the goal is to clear your mind completely. Allow yourself to become calm and relaxed. Feel the earth under your feet and focus on your breathing. As thoughts come up, acknowledge them and let them go. Spend time appreciating being alive and find something about which to feel good.

After 10 minutes of walking like this, I find that whatever I need to focus most on in my life bubbles to the top of my mind. As this happens, I allow myself to consider these thoughts in a calm way. As the thoughts come up, I allow them to roll around in my mind so that new ways of approaching a challenge are considered, and new energy to address them starts to flow. I make a mental note of any actions I plan to take and then allow the next thought to bubble up. Sometimes I can develop amazing solutions to tough problems just by allowing my thoughts to flow.

As I allow my mind to think in a deep and calm manner, I also acknowledge my talents and abilities. I take the time to feel good about any of my accomplishments. I get in touch with the positive source of energy that flows into my body, from the universe and penetrates all things. As I do this, a renewed energy begins to surge through my body. I feel a swirling ball of warm vitality in my chest and head. I allow this feeling to fill up any emotional hole that I may have been feeling inside my body.

To end my walking meditation, I again revisit any deep thoughts or action steps that bubbled up during the process. When I return, I write down any meaningful thoughts, actions, or ideas that came to me during the process. Once my actions are written, I immediately begin to work on them.

Writing them down ensures that, when completed, I get the satisfaction of crossing them off my list.

THE HIGH PRICE OF BEING NORMAL

There is a powerful cultural message that we should strive to be like everyone else, that it is wise to fit in, and that being different is a situation to avoid. This message is encouraged by advertising and media that glorify the joys of using the same products and services. If you are different in any way, either physically or socially, they have a fix for that, too. Some businesses promise to help you fit in, by masking your flaws or eccentricities. There is safety in staying with the herd. Few want to be singled out for being unaware of social trends, fashion, or even thinking differently.

Although being mainstream is comfortable and safe, does it have a cost? Is there a price to be paid for running with the pack? I say YES in a big way. Statistics indicate that 95% of us stay in our comfort zone and, therefore, achieve an average life. The other 5% are willing to get out of their comfort zone, be different, and take risks. These people achieve far more than most. They have wealth, fame, and great adventures. They have stopped caring what others think of them and have started caring more about what they think of themselves. They have refused to accept less than greatness. They have accepted themselves for who they are with all their flaws. They understand that many things cannot be controlled, but they have made sure to change what they could.

Consider this: many people are not even living for themselves. They are living the life that others wanted for them. The life their parents, friends, teachers, or the media said would be good for them. They are motivated by outside, often negative, influences that guide them to places they did not choose. How many of us have taken the time to figure out what we want? Moreover, how many of us have then taken the actions to get it? On the other hand, are we like a ship without a rudder, being pushed around the ocean by the wind through the influences of TV, social media, the news, and "friends" who mean well. How many of us have ever taken steps to control our environmental influences and affect the sailing direction of our lives?

I contend that the obvious price of being normal is mediocrity. Being normal in Western culture means spending most of your time exposed to the negative influences of TV news, radio, friends, and social networks. It means that you are living in an environment that does not support success, freethinking, and positive ideas. The card deck is stacked against you.

Advertisers figured out a long time ago that we are easily manipulated, distracted, and enticed into buying stuff. We enjoy spending time watching shocking shows and people behaving badly on TV and the Internet. Moreover, this manipulation could be done in a way that we wouldn't even notice how we were losing our individuality and our precious time. Ultimately, we would fail to recognize we had lost our ability to think freely and rise above the crowd.

If this is true, then what can you do about it? First, recognize that distractions in your life are the enemy. They will rob you of your time, resources, and goals. Most media is just a negative distraction. For example, how do you feel after watching the TV news? Did it raise your spirit and give you hope for a better life? For me it never does, and this goes for most media. Sometimes it makes me sick to my stomach. It may be fascinating, but being informed of all the problems in the world will not benefit your outlook on life.

What if we could take back control of our media environment? Back from the broadcasters with their manipulation of fear, violence, greed, and sex. What if we started exposing ourselves to what is right in the world, instead of what's wrong with it? I decided to do this for myself a couple of years ago. I virtually stopped watching network TV, decided to read only the news headlines online, and began to expose myself to positive messages and music on a regular basis. I built a library of inspiring speakers, comedy shows, and uplifting music that I could play in my car, on my phone, and my computer. In this serene environment, I stayed focused on my goals, began feeling good, building relationships, taking action and risks, and living my dreams. I began programming my life for success.

There is a new breed of online media you can use to control your environment and stay focused and positive. For example, I helped create a streaming Internet radio station called **Program Your Life Radio (PYL Radio)**. It has motivational speakers, easy listening music, and much more. When I listen, it allows me to control my influences and program myself for success and happiness. Anyone can listen to PYL Radio; the station is free.

Remember; leaders are different. They enjoy standing out in the crowd and challenging rules. They are focusing on the positive and creating, instead of criticizing. They are uninspired with normalcy and seek a different path.

So stop being normal because normal is boring. Do something today to take back control over your life and end the negative distractions that are robbing you of success and happiness. One small change can make a huge difference over a lifetime.

CHAPTER SUMMARY

As a chosen one novice, you have the opportunity to choose yourself for greatness and become aware of the limiting beliefs and habits that may have held you back.

The novice also learns to take responsibility for where they are in life, regardless of the circumstances that led them there. The time for blame and shame has passed because those choices don't create the type of learning necessary for true growth. The novice also observes how the mind makes up false negative stories about the future. They learn to ignore these mind tricks or exert control over them by changing them to positive stories that add to motivation.

The novice begins to understand the power of fear and how it may have stopped them in the past. The novice also chooses their values and learns to apply them in their decision-making. Relationships are important to the novice, and they actively work to repair and strengthen them or remove them.

Finally, the novice understands and celebrates their joys and strengths and uses them to benefit themselves and the world. They value and enhance their health and focus on living in the now instead of the past and future. The novice has fully accepted who they are and is excited about their future.

You will know you are ready to proceed to an apprentice when you have taken full responsibility for your life, chosen your values, and forgiven yourself for the past. Blaming others and being ashamed or angry about your past must be released here. You cannot change anything you do not believe you control. Once we accept responsibility for what we have become, then we are in the position to change ourselves.

Choosing myself for greatness was not an easy task for me. Born a middle child, I was not accustomed to being in the spotlight and tended to want to lead from the center. When I participated in a 90 goal setting program, my nickname was the "Invisible Man" because I was so quiet. It meant taking responsibility for this characteristic and working to change it. It was in conflict with what I wanted, and I had to let go of the story that I was not a leader since it no longer served me. After this, I began to add my name and face to my websites and blogs.

Even more important for me was forgiveness. My previous mistakes and lack of success had resulted in a self-loathing that manifested as self-sabotage in my goal setting. Deep down I didn't like myself even though I appeared positive on the outside. It also showed up in unhealthy habits such as poor eating, negative story making, lack of exercise, and low self-worth.

Self-forgiveness can only be accomplished by getting in touch with your emotional side. I had to relive the traumas of my past and find empathy for myself. Change my perception and accept that I did the best I could at the time. By doing this repeatedly, I could release my self-judgments and regain a view of my inner self as innocent and worthy.

Releasing my self-judgments and gaining forgiveness has been the most rewarding personal development work of my life. I not only regained respect for myself but also for others where I had held grudges.

When you have truly forgiven and accepted yourself the hard work of personal development is over. You will no longer sabotage or fail to believe in yourself, and the process ahead will be easy. A word of caution, most people never get this far. They hold on to past offenses and lament their shortcomings. So if you struggle with the steps ahead come back to this chapter and practice forgiveness.

As a review, the steps a novice will go through are listed below.
1. Choose yourself for greatness
2. Forgive yourself

3. Take responsibility
4. Choose your values
5. Remove negative influences
6. Health evaluation
7. Don't make up stories
8. Meditation walking
9. The high price of being normal.

10

~~~~~~~

APPRENTICE

THE APPRENTICE

The purpose of the apprentice level is to set future goals and a life purpose based on your values. You get to recreate yourself as you always wanted.

As a novice and initiate you looked into the past and present for knowledge about how you arrived at your current place in life. You should now have a better understanding of your strengths and weaknesses and what you want to improve. You should also be aware of how the mind can work both for and against you. We acknowledged the past because before you can embark on a new course for yourself, it is important to know your starting position.

Now we will release the past and start to look into your future. This is your chance to begin to recreate your life the way you always wanted it to be. You will cast aside any old limiting beliefs and design a bold future for yourself as the star of your own reality show. You get to take center stage and see your name up in lights. If what you desire can be imagined, it can be realized.

At the apprentice attainment level, you get to decide what you want and set goals for your new future. You get an opportunity to recreate yourself and develop belief you can obtain it. You will include joy and fun in your goals, and they will be in alignment with your values. Do not worry about how they will materialize. Just set the goals and allow the universe to figure out the best method. Your goals will be put into action as a journeyman.

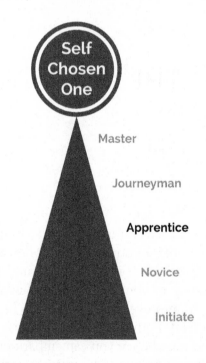

Here you will learn to care more about what you think rather than others opinions and become grateful for what you already have. You will start to believe it is possible for you to have what you want and make a decision to live in faith instead of fear. You will foster your own self-value and self-concept. You will realize and accept that inconvenience is the price of success.

You will set and begin to take action on your goals and be willing to make and even encourage mistakes as part of the learning process. Things are about to get exciting, so start thinking about what you want your future to look like.

SELF-VALUE, SELF-CONCEPT, I AM CONCEPT

Let's start again by looking at your current beliefs. How would you describe yourself to someone else? What would you tell them about yourself? For example, would you say "I am a writer, a husband, a father, a brother, a teacher?" Perhaps you would say, "I am a mother, daughter, sister, entrepreneur, an artist." Describe yourself right now and see what you come up with:

I AM_____

For many people the words they use to describe themselves are very limited. They may think they are humble, but these limited words describe a limited life. For most, their self-concept and self-value are low. As one of the chosen ones, your goal is to expand your self-concept. To do this, make a list of who you want to be and put it in the present form. Use words such as I am... Once your list is complete, a good habit is to say these I AM statements to yourself every day. See a small list of mine below. When I first made my list, it was quite small.

- I am a leader of self.
- I am a giver.
- I am healthier.
- I am intelligent.
- I am motivated.
- I am always growing.
- I am wealthier.
- I am proud of myself and others.
- I am limitless.
- I am confident.
- I am excited about my life.
- I am free of stress.

- I am eating healthy every day.
- I am well rested.
- I am willing to take risks.
- I am aware that success lies on the other side of failure.
- I am persistent.
- I am learning to fly.
- I am feeling good.
- I am happy with my body.
- I am resourceful.
- I am more loving.
- I am fun loving .
- I am happier.
- I am not in resistance to what is.
- I am flexible and limber.
- I am ready to make a change in my life.
- I am unselfish with my love and attention.
- I am athletic.
- I am amazing.

Repeating I AM statements on a regular basis will actually help rebuild your self-esteem. The positive routine you develop will replace negative thoughts and enhance the way you describe and think of yourself. Do it and see what happens. Your self-concept is how you see yourself and what you think you are capable of accomplishing.

Chosen ones choose to let go of the past and create a bright future for themselves and others. Your past is not who you are. It is who you were. You are who you believe you are from this day forward. You are what you say to yourself. You are how you describe yourself. Begin to describe yourself as who you wish to be. Write a new I AM statement below and make it better than the first one above.

I AM_____

BELIEVE IT IS POSSIBLE FOR YOU

You are worthy of your goals and dreams. No one is worth more, and no one is worth less than you are. Your very existence means you're worthy of anything your mind can imagine. You are capable of becoming anything. The people in the world that have what you want are no better than you are. Feelings of not being enough can be overcome.

Who is your spiritual, business, or artistic idol? Who do you look up to and want to be like? Take a second to bring someone to mind. Now, imagine having your idol as your friend or colleague. How do you feel about working together with them on a new project, business, or venture? Why *not* you?

The skills, knowledge, and desire are within you. They need new partners and the ideas and skills you possess. People with creative ideas and imagination are scarce in this world. Just look at all the terrible movie sequels that attempt to piggyback on the creativity of the first one.

Begin to imagine that successful people and companies need you and not the other way around. They are looking for your talents and abilities. They need to continue to innovate to stay successful. Their need gives you power, something of value to offer, and a negotiating position. Did you know when you value yourself highly others do the same?

When approaching desirable people and companies, do so as a potential business partner and not as an employee. Employees give all their good ideas to the company freely, whereas partners are paid highly for the ideas they contribute. You do not need experience to do this, just ideas, skills, and courage.

The same is true for starting your own company or becoming an artist, speaker, or author. The world needs and wants what you have to contribute. You are bringing something unique and valuable to the marketplace. Take your ideas and self seriously when you create your product or service goals because the market will pay you highly for them. Begin to believe anything is possible for you because it is.

BECOME GRATEFUL

How much do you appreciate the overall quality of your current life? Keep in mind all lives have elements of both good and bad. Do you have a tendency to focus on one or the other? In my experience, most of us focus on what we do not like about our lives. We see the flaws and focus on improving them, which can be a good behavior. However, we may also ignore the good life we already have by focusing exclusively on the bad parts. Do you know someone like this?

The Law of Attraction is a concept, about which many personal development books and speakers love to talk. Roughly, it states, that which we focus upon grows stronger, and that which we ignore grows weaker. If this is true, then focusing on our flaws is counterproductive. Instead, we should focus exclusively on what is good in our lives, and make that grow.

So, we focus on what's good because we want more of it, don't we? Based on my research, we do it through the mindset and practice of gratefulness. Gratefulness is both a mindset and a set of practices; the mindset tells us to focus on what is working instead of what is not, and the practice is where we acknowledge what we are grateful for through meditation, prayer, or by making periodic gratitude lists.

Let's explore the mindset of gratefulness first. Using the mindset of gratefulness, we begin to think of everything we have in our lives as a gift. We give thanks to all our friends, family, and acquaintances. We give thanks for everything that we enjoy in our lives such as possessions and events. We allow ourselves to feel good about what we already have.

This sends a signal to the universe; we want more of this. By leveraging the law of attraction, we focus on what is good and then it grows due to our focusing on it. When we do this as a matter of habit, we start to become more positive and see the good in everything. We see potential in others instead of flaws. We see hope instead of despair. We see ways to success instead of ways of failure.

A key concept is that we consider all events as gifts even if they appear to be bad at first. We shift our thinking to believe that within every event, task, or challenge, there is a hidden benefit that we will later come to understand. As Marshall Thurber says, "Everything's perfect, I just don't see it yet."

So when something happens you think is bad, you can start by saying, "That's good." Once you say it, then your mind will begin to look for the evidence of this. You may see it right away as a new opportunity or skill you will develop. On the other hand, the realization may come later once things have become clearer.

As an example, I received a job offer to work for Microsoft in the late 1990's. I had always wanted to work for this company, and they finally made me an offer. I consulted with my family about the decision and realized it would triple my commuting time and lengthen my office hours. After I considered how little time, I would have with my small children at home, and the possible negative effect on my marriage, I decided to turn down the offer.

At first, I was disappointed that I passed on this great opportunity. It would have been a tremendous addition to my resume and experience. However, over the years, I have come to realize how lucky I was to say no. The commute would have made my workdays 12 hours long. I would not have been able to spend time with my young boys and coach their soccer teams.

I would not have been able to keep my relationship with my wife strong. She would hardly have seen me during the week. We would only see each other on the weekends. As I learned, there is a popular expression used to describe the wives of Microsoft employees – Microsoft "widows." They rarely see their husbands and often end up divorced. Saying no to that job saved my relationship with my boys and my marriage – that's good.

Moving to the practice of gratefulness, integrates grateful thinking into your everyday life. You can set up a daily practice to reinforce the mindset. My wife often does this at night before she goes to sleep. There are several other ways to do this. In fact, there are whole books devoted just to this topic. One way to implement it is discussed here.

This practice is usually done in the evening or at the end of the day. It can be done with a notepad or journal and is performed freehand. You start by turning to a clean page and writing at the top of it, "I am grateful for." Then, you begin making a list of all the people, places, events, and things you are grateful to have in your life.

I usually start with people first. My family is a hugely positive part of my life. My wife and my sons, who have now become young men, always bring me joy. I also include my parents, whether living or not, and maybe even mention something they taught me. My siblings and extended family also make the list.

From there I may add my home, sometimes my job or co-workers, and places that I love to go. The simple pleasures of life such as good coffee, a warm fire, or a sunny day can be added. Any events that I wish to celebrate, I add to the list. I write birthdays, holidays, graduations, promotions, raises, and good workouts on the list. I also put possessions that make me happy on my list, such as my car, a comfortable chair, or my motorcycle.

The list does not have to be long, and I don't recommend you always include the same people, places, events, and things on it each day. It just takes five minutes to write down whatever comes to mind that you are grateful for now. If you do this just before bedtime, you will go to sleep thinking happy and positive thoughts. This will undoubtedly improve your sleep.

Write down a few things you are grateful for right now. This will enhance the appreciation of what you already have.

I am grateful for_____

In summary, gratefulness is a mindset that you can acquire both through practice and by focusing on what you want, as opposed to what you don't. It is a characteristic that all chosen ones employ to help them focus their minds. By practicing it every day, you are activating the law of attraction in your favor. Start your practice of gratefulness tonight.

FORGIVE OTHERS

One important step along the journey of the chosen ones is to forgive yourself and others. Here is a shocking fact. Whether we know it or not, most of us have not forgiven others or ourselves for things in our past. Most of us hold grudges for mistakes, physical deficiencies, and personality flaws even if they are beyond our control.

In the Book *Forgive to Win*, the author, Walter Jacobson, describes how most people have self-loathing and that is why they sabotage their lives. They have a low inner opinion of themselves and believe they don't deserve success or are unworthy. This manifests as self-sabotage as they attempt to achieve success in life. What a revelation this was for me and the only fix for this is self-forgiveness.

How is this done? Walter Jacobson says that self-sabotage can be overcome by withholding judgments and by forgiving others first. You see, when we judge others, we are actually judging ourselves at the same time. Judgment is the process in which we compare someone to a standard, or to ourselves. These standards are typically unreachable such as being constantly in fashion, beautiful, kind, correct, or smart. Nobody can ever meet the standard, including ourselves.

So our judgments of others come back to haunt us because we know that we cannot meet them either. This creates self-loathing. How often do we judge others? In my experience, we are constantly judging others, and often harshly. We can learn to withhold these judgments, or judge kindly to overcome this trap. Thus, as we accept others flaws, we make our flaws acceptable, and we can forgive our shortcomings.

To forgive ourselves we must forgive others first since it is difficult to forgive ourselves directly. The good news is that every act of forgiveness makes us more forgivable. Who do you need to forgive? Did you know that withholding forgiveness hurts you more? Hanging on to negative thoughts about another person focuses our mind on this.

We do not feel good about ourselves when we fail to forgive another as well. We are still in judgment of that person. As I have described, this judgment of others turns against us. When we cannot forgive others and ourselves, we will continue to sabotage our lives. We can overcome this.

We can learn to forgive completely. Few people fully understand this. Many people may say they have forgiven, but in truth, they have not. The true meaning of forgiveness is to, give as before. How many of us truly give as before the offense occurred? I think many of us give less and then watch that person more closely than before. We trust them less and may treat them unkindly in the future even after we have said we forgave them.

We can practice letting go of our judgments and giving as before to forgive others and ourselves. We can speak kindly of others and overlook their flaws. We can accept others flaws and then truly accept our own. Read *Forgive to Win* for more information on this. It is a short, powerful book.

Conceive-Believe-Achieve

Amazingly, success is a predictable thing. The people who study it, learn the skills and techniques, and then put them into practice in their lives are consistently successful. The people who think that success is based on luck, position, heritage, ruthlessness, or athletic skill will not even bother to study it. They don't think it is possible, and that makes them unable to obtain it.

From my research, the factors to success are very simple, and anyone is capable of understanding them and taking the necessary actions. In fact, the factors to success are not even secrets. The steps have been revealed many times. They are obvious and simple, although most people fail to grasp the power of simple things.

The steps are remembered using initials as easy as ABC. The letters ABC do contain the formula, but it is more often ordered as CBA or Conceive-Believe-Achieve. The first letter C stands for Conceive. It means conceive what you want. See it in your imagination. See it in detail. Imagine the result of what you want. Is it a business, a home, a car, greater wealth, more love, or better health? Whatever it is, conceive it in your mind with as much clarity as you can create. This is the step of creation.

As Mike Dooley says, "Thoughts become things," and these things need to exist in your mind before they will ever exist in the real world. So become single-minded and focused on what you want. You may want multiple things but focusing on one thing at a time is much more powerful than scattered focus. I have heard that most people get only to the step of conceiving. To increase your chances of success write down what you want, draw it in pictures, or make a vision board and you'll do even better, according to the famous time management author, Brian Tracy.

Next is the letter B, which stands for Believe. This means you must believe you can have what you want and believe that it is possible for you especially. Even believe that you already have it. This is where most people stop in the process. They may think, what's the point of believing in something that doesn't exist? On the other hand, I can't just make this stuff up! The point is that unless you believe you are worthy of what you want, you will always sabotage yourself and fail to get it. Any actions you take will be half steps, feeble attempts, tries instead of do's. Your willpower will be weak and so will your results.

You create a belief that you already have it so that your subconscious mind will accept your worthiness of it. Without this belief, when you fail it will be because of some made up excuses such as resources, time, money, connections, tactics, and skills. These excuses will always mask the truth that you didn't fully commit. You never thought it was possible for you and you never truly believed. When you see yourself as already having it, then you know you deserve it, and you feel the feeling of having it. That feeling is vital because you can't have what you can't feel.

Did you know self-worth comes from feelings, not thoughts? Thoughts can create rationalizations and options, but feelings actually make decisions and build self-esteem. Therefore, when you change your feelings about what you deserve, your decisions will change. Then, when your decisions change, your results will change, and when your results change, your level of success will increase dramatically.

The final letter is A which stands for Achieve. Achieve is synonymous with action. Once you believe your goal is possible, the actions necessary will be taken by you naturally and easily so you will achieve it. Of course, you must believe that you actually deserve it. Many people think that you must Achieve before you Believe, but that is not the proper order. Belief must come before Achievement is possible. Belief is what drives you forward. Belief is what makes you strong, persistent, consistent, and resourceful. Belief naturally brings together the money, relationships, and skills needed. Belief means that if one tactic or method doesn't work, you just do another.

Any mistakes made along the way become feedback that you need to adjust your strategy. Mistakes mean nothing about your self-worth, they are just good information to sharpen your skills. Did you know actions driven by strong belief have amazing power and effectiveness? Actions taken, driven by belief, demonstrate real leadership and everyone is inspired to support a leader. People naturally follow people who believe in themselves and are taking bold action. Boldness comes as the result of true belief.

To review, the factors to success are as simple as ABC or more specifically CBA. Conceive your goal or dream, Believe you deserve it, and Achieve it through bold action. The specific actions you take, do not need to be effective at first, and you will make mistakes. Mistakes are good because they provide the feedback needed to find the win-win solutions of success. Therefore, the process of Conceive, Believe, and Achieve is the simple solution to success. Is this solution too simple for you? Some people have a need for complicated solutions. Don't over-complicate things. Grasp this easy process and success will be yours.

DECIDE WHAT YOU WANT

Creating or recreating yourself is really about deciding what you want, and who you need to become to get it. You begin by conceiving your goals and dreams. The process of Conceive-Believe-Achieve applies here. You are going to conceive what you want, believe you can have it, and then go out and achieve it based on that belief. This simple process is used in several professional 90-day goal programs. They all start with a goal setting exercise, so let us go through one now.

Goals need to be set in several areas. First, professional goals such as wealth, starting a business, getting a raise or promotion, or increasing revenues, should be made. Second, emotional goals such as improving a relationship, finding a mate, or making amends, are made. Third, physical goals such as improving health or increasing exercise are very helpful. Fourth, make a spiritual goal such as starting a practice of meditation, joining a cause, or beginning spiritual study.

To start the process, you pick goals in at least three of these areas and write them down on paper. As we stated earlier, goals written down have more power and are more likely to be obtained than stated goals. Goals that use the SMART acronym are more effective. The acronym stands for Specific, Measurable, Actionable, Risky, and Time-bound. Time-bound means that goals need to have a target date to be truly effective.

As an apprentice, it is time for you to recreate yourself and set big goals as the way to start. Use the space below to define four SMART goals that once attained will change your life. If the goal is not life changing, then it is not big enough. If you have done it previously, this is not a good goal either. Good goals are usually things we do not know how to do and are a bit scary to think about. So think huge and do not put any limits on yourself because you can have anything you desire.

Write your goals here once you have conceived them. Give them a timeframe such as one year, or six months, or by June of 2019. Do not read any further in the book until you have picked your big goals.

Professional_____

Emotional_____

Physical_____

Spiritual_____

The goals you chose above, if you took the opportunity and some risk, could be the turning point in your life. Next, you will want to commit to making them happen and see them as already accomplished. If they bring up fear, then you chose well. If not, then revise them until they do. As a journeyman, you will begin to put these goals into action.

I encourage you to take this opportunity to choose some new huge goals to achieve in your life. Just go for it, and you don't need to have any idea how you will achieve them. Do not play it safe. Ordinary goals will lead to ordinary results, and you probably have that already.

DEFINE YOUR HIGHER PURPOSE

Refer to your chosen goals and think about how they relate to a higher purpose in life. The best goals are in alignment with a higher purpose or perhaps more than one. For example, a goal of opening a restaurant is in alignment with the higher purpose of feeding the world high-quality food. A goal of becoming a doctor is in alignment with caring for the sick.

Having goals that are in alignment with a higher purpose will make them more powerful. Goal seekers are naturally more motivated to work for a cause greater than themselves. Also, other people are more likely to assist you with your goals when they fulfill a greater need in the world. There are many higher purposes such as world peace, feeding the hungry, ending domestic violence, equality, social justice, happiness, personal development, and ending poverty.

Every worthy goal is in alignment with a higher purpose. Take time to figure out what your higher purpose truly is, based upon your goals. This is your true purpose in life.

Write it down below. If you have more than one, write them all down.

Higher Purpose(s)_____

Once you know your higher purpose, other ideas and goals may materialize. As a doctor, you may invent a new drug or procedure that fixes a previously untreatable condition. This is in alignment with a higher purpose and expands the original vision. Having a higher purpose will give your goals more power and energy. It will help you convince people and yourself of their value. It is critical to tie what you want to a higher purpose.

Knowing your higher purpose may also change some of your goals. If you need to modify your goals from the last section, do it now before moving on.

TRANSFORM YOUR ENVIRONMENT

The environment in which we live has a strong effect on our results and our outlook on the world. Our environment includes the places we live and work, our friends and family, our music, TV shows, activities, hobbies, and social networks. When was the last time you considered the supportiveness of your current environment? Does it improve your odds of getting what you want, or not?

An unhealthy or negative environment can be tough to overcome. It can keep you stuck in a negative mindset and performing activities that are not helpful to long-term success. Unknowingly, you may be contributing to this process by maintaining attachments to negative things, events, people, and places. Can you think of any?

The good news is that your environment can be transformed into a positive and supportive place filled with people who love and support you. You don't have to stay in your current environment if it has become unproductive or toxic. The first step is letting go of the things, places, and people who have a negative influence on you. This is easier than you may think.

To make room for positive and supportive influences, you must first get rid of the old memories that can haunt you. Do you have old clothes you don't enjoy wearing or that do not fit anymore? Do you have household items that remind you of old, bitter memories? Keeping them around just holds you back and keeps you stuck. So, get rid of any clothes that you don't love to wear. Replacing your clothes is not that expensive and, if you are like me, you probably have more than you need.

This holds true for household items as well. Do you have furniture, pictures, lamps, books, or any other items in your house that bring up bad memories? If so, it's time to clean them out to make room for newer items that make you feel great about yourself. You must let go of the past to make room for a better future. Give them away or have a yard sale.

You may have a tendency to hang on to items from your past even if they make you feel lousy. Getting rid of these things is not denying your past; it is freeing you from your past. Letting go of the past means that it will no longer define you. Your new future will look completely different from your past. It will be so much better you will no longer need stuff from another era.

Transforming your environment means that you may also reevaluate your choices in music, TV, radio, and social media. Did you know that many of the mainstream media choices are not supportive of growth and achievement? Instead, they are designed to occupy your mind with minutia, sex, greed, and keep you watching others live their dreams while you sit on the sidelines.

Did you know that many sources of motivational media can replace the negative mainstream choices? Many of these can be found on the Internet in the form of streaming radio and TV stations, downloadable podcasts, webinars, and meet-up groups. You can even obtain CDs and listen to positive media in the car.

Did you know that most successful people learn about and talk about ideas, not other people? New ideas are what excite them and make them profitable. Everyone else talks about and focuses on people. They are concerned about who said what, what the celebs are doing, and the constant drama that the news loves to broadcast. Consider most TV and news shows; they are all about people, and who is to blame. Get off the popular media hamster wheel.

How do you feel about your present job? Do you love it, despise it, or just bored with it? Your job has a huge impact on your environment. You should constantly be looking for ways to improve the way you use your working hours. The job that pays more money is not always the one that will be most satisfying. Focus on satisfying work, not just income. It feels better.

Since our jobs take so much of our time, it is important that we enjoy them. If you have lost the passion for your job, then find a way to change it. Sometimes you can take a lateral position that is much more rewarding. You may be able to take on new tasks and responsibilities and alter your job for the better. Otherwise, start looking for a new career, business, or job that excites you. Life is too short to work at something that you don't enjoy.

A great way to transform your environment is to get a mentor. A mentor is someone that already has knowledge, skill, and success in the areas of life that you want to improve. The fast movers in society all have powerful mentors. Having a mentor will vastly shorten the time it takes to be successful. My mentor was greatly responsible for helping me create this book.

Some mentors will do it for free if you have a family relationship or job affiliation. However, in my experience, you have to compensate mentors for their time because their time is so valuable and the time they spend with you could be used for many other productive purposes.

So plan to compensate your mentor because the time you spend with them will more than cover the costs. There are many mentors available in almost every industry. You can find them through professional associations, the Internet, seminars, and classes. Often the teacher of any professional course has a mentoring or coaching program.

A mentoring program will provide you with contacts, resources, ideas, and motivation that you could not otherwise obtain. Some even have mastermind groups that bring together their best and brightest students. These are your prime candidates for business relationships, jobs, and partnerships.

Another great way to transform your home environment is to create a vision board for your goals and post it where you can see it every day. My wife and I do this every year or two. We put pictures of places we want to visit on a poster board along with key goals and phrases. We also put images that represent our goals such as beautiful homes, cars, and healthy people who are leading active lives.

I have mine on the bedroom wall and see it as I head to the shower each morning. Some of the goals on my current board are physical fitness, travel, charity, self-discipline, fun, wealth, and persistence. I also have photos of two people I admire: Robert Kiyosaki and Warren Buffett. I update my vision board regularly. It is a fun and creative way to change your home environment.

Another way to enhance your environment is to create a sacred space for yourself to create and learn. A place in your home where you can be alone and focus on your goals, study, embrace your gifts and meditate. To prepare a space for this, ensure it is clean and free of distractions such as TV and loud noises. This is a good place to hang your vision board and your goals list.

You may also light candles in this space while you are there. I keep ashes from a fire walk that I did last year. In this area, place furniture and items that make you feel good and add to the creative process. Make a daily routine to spend at least one hour a day in this space doing activities that create real world solutions. Remember, although this is a relaxing place, it is not a place for distractions such as video games or TV.

Once you have a sacred space, you can begin to use it for any productive purpose you desire. This place will always help you feel good about yourself. When you feel good, you are better able to tap into your creativity.

ENCOURAGE MISTAKES

Are you afraid to make mistakes? Are you afraid to look stupid? Are you unable to make decisions quickly? Are you a reluctant leader? Do you look to others for the "right" way to accomplish tasks? If so, then you are the way I used to be. You see, I was taught always to have the "right" answer. In school and at home I watched and learned that mistakes were "bad" and you didn't want to make them. The consequences were looking ignorant, shame, blame, and fear. I learned to sit back and watch instead of taking the lead.

My fragile self-esteem was based on the results of my actions. If I made a mistake, it meant I was inferior, not just someone who was learning a new skill. Of course, this was not true. It was just a story I made up about what mistakes meant, but it felt real.

What I have realized is that mistakes are just how we learn. They are neither good nor bad, and they don't say anything about who I am or my value. When I was a little boy, I made many mistakes. I fell often, and I learned to walk and then ride a bike. I said words incorrectly when I learned to speak. I smashed two words together and made new ones. My parents just laughed and enjoyed the process of watching me grow.

Through these mistakes, I received the information I needed to master new skills. The feedback was valuable, and I could not have learned any other way. So why is it that as adults, some of us decide that making mistakes is bad, and we become uncomfortable with making them? Doesn't this just mean that we have stopped learning?

I have come to understand that there is no right or wrong way to do anything. There are a variety of methods to accomplish tasks. Some of them may be more efficient, but that doesn't make the others wrong. The connotation of right and wrong is just a judgment we put on things. This is unnecessary and just keeps us from moving forward. How many times have we failed to take action on our goals because we didn't want to do it wrong?

How are we supposed to know how to do it if we can't make any mistakes along the way? That's the way we learn, isn't it? If we are so focused on doing it right, then we will never take any action. Our fears will creep up and take away our dreams long before we can move towards them. Mistakes are neutral because they are just information.

We must be willing to be bad at something, at first, to become good at it later. One of my favorite quotes is "Dare to suck!" In other words, dare to be crappy at any new thing you want to do. Then, take the feedback you receive and become better.

Release any judgment of yourself and others' mistakes. Judgment of others is the same as judgment of ourselves. When we judge others, we put those same limitations on ourselves. What would you rather have, a life of freedom of expression or a life of limitations? I choose freedom, and when we stop being in judgment, we open ourselves to becoming free.

Some great advice I got from a seminar was to make as many mistakes as fast as I could because that's the best way to learn. With that kind of attitude, I'm either on the winning team or the learning team—there is no losing team. Either way, I am a worthy person living a life of discovery and growing every day. That's the way I choose to live, and I recommend it to you.

INTELLECTUAL PROPERTY IS KEY

In the era of the Internet, one business strategy works better than all others. It's a strategy that provides leverage, dynamic value, and is rigorously protected in the western world. If you are using any other strategy as a basis for your business, then you will be at a big disadvantage in the 21st century and beyond. This top business strategy for the future involves using intellectual property.

Intellectual property (IP) is the ultimate business strategy for the modern world. It has legal protections that, in some cases, last for nearly 100 years, and the United States recently extended protections on copyrights. IP is largely intangible, so it is perfect for distribution that leverages the Internet. There are many examples of this such as music, eBooks, video, webinars, reports, and online training classes.

IP contains an immense amount of dynamic value. People are drawn to the valuable content, and it is easy to modify and keep current. Dynamic value makes you unique, and higher than normal prices can be charged.

What is intellectual property (IP)? There are four foundations of IP: patents, copyrights, trademarks, and rights of publicity. Each type has its own legal protections and advantages. For the purpose of this book, I will focus on copyrights since they are easy to leverage by the non-technically educated.

What is a copyright? Copyright protects a literary, musical, dramatic, choreographic, pictorial or graphic, audiovisual, architectural work, or sound recording, from being reproduced without the permission of the copyright owner.

The owner has the right to transfer the copyright to another party if they choose. In the United States, this right lasts for the life of the author plus 50 years; or in the case of a copyright held by an entity, such as a business, for 75 years.

To hold a copyright, you must be a creator of unique content such as music, video, books, blogs, graphics, art, performance, or audio. Once you create these items, they become your dynamic value legally protected by the copyright. You are then free to sell your content in any way you wish, such as on the Internet.

The main advantage of IP through a copyright is that you create the content one time and then can sell or distribute it as many times are you wish cheaply. Copyrighted items can be distributed via CDs. DVDs, books, video tapes, eBooks, or downloaded in various file formats.

This gives IP a superior profit margin over tangible products that must be manufactured, inventoried, transported, warehoused, and sold by retailers who take about 50% of the profits.

Content can be copyright protected for a nominal fee of about $35 in the United States. Filing a formal copyright is recommended, although, under U.S. copyright law, a work is automatically protected by copyright when it is created. However, this law should not be fully relied on for copyright protection or enforcement should you need to take civil action against a copyright infringer.

Being the owner of copyrighted content puts you in the driver's seat for success. It is highly protected by law, creates dynamic value, and can be easily leveraged. Many forms of business rely on IP, so there is bound to be one that makes you excited.

Creating dynamic value using IP is the starting point to using almost all other proven strategies. This is where the journey to success begins and where the magic happens. Once your dynamic value is created, you can then deploy the other business strategies to transform it into wealth.

A great attribute of IP is that you can always create more of it or improve it. It is a source of unlimited value without scarcity. The only limit is your imagination and creativity. Begin taking your ideas and creating your own dynamic value right now. Do it in your spare time if you already have a job.

In my opinion, you must be an owner of IP to master the road to success. It is the greatest business strategy of our time.

DECIDE TO BE INCONVENIENCED

Inconvenience has killed more dreams than just about anything else because it is inconvenient to follow through on your dreams and goals. Taking time for others is inconvenient. It is inconvenient to get out of your comfort zone and take the risks that will be necessary for success. How many opportunities have you missed due to inconvenience?

I have missed lots of them because opportunities come at unusual times. They conflict with existing obligations and schedules. They sometimes require us to give up existing routines and activities we enjoy. Just face it. Your future success will require lots of inconveniences.

Here is an example, in 2013, I enrolled in a 90-day goal setting, and leadership team course held by the Personal Success Institute (PSI Seminars). At that time, I was working full time and supporting my family of four. I was playing soccer two days a week and team captain on one of my teams. I also played fantasy football in two leagues. In short, I already had a busy life.

Once the 90-day program started, I had to make difficult choices because I needed time to work on my goals. Therefore, I gave up being soccer team captain and stopped playing on one of the teams. Fantasy football became less important to me, and my football teams all tanked that year.

I began working evenings and weekends on my goals and had to travel out of town for four-weekend activities. I spent one night a week with my new goal setting team, supporting them while they supported me. It was a lot of change that was not easy, as it was very inconvenient and out of my comfort zone.

However, here is what I created due to being inconvenienced. First, I committed to and exercised 45 minutes per day, which led to weight loss and lower blood pressure.

Second, I built a 25' x 15' concrete patio and retaining wall in my yard, so my wife and I had the entertaining space we had always dreamed of having. We spent our mornings on this patio having coffee and talking about our dreams. Third, my wife and I read a relationship book together aloud, which brought us closer. I highly suggest every couple read *Men are from Mars and Women are from Venus*. We have a new and better understanding of each other and now rate our relationship at a 10 out of 10 points.

Fourth, I created a personal growth streaming Internet radio station called Program Your Life Radio. Its goal is to create a streaming audio environment of hope, courage, support, peace, abundance, knowledge, and dreams. It includes lectures, music, comedy, and meditations to inspire your soul. You see, I believe we need to create new positive media environments to counteract the existing negative media, which panders to greed, violence, scarcity, and fear. To do this, I contacted and enrolled several major motivational and inspirational speakers for the station. I had never done anything like this before and had no idea how to accomplish it.

Through the support of my team and coaches, I brought my vision into the world. The station now has several well-known inspirational speakers, listeners in more than 40 countries around the world, and is still growing. My wife and I also co-host a podcast called the *Program Your Life Podcast*, where we share what is working for us. The journey has been riddled with inconvenience, but the results have been more than worthwhile.

Once you decide that inconvenience is necessary and helpful, you will open yourself to greater success. Here is a tip. Interrupt your existing routines and schedules when opportunities arise and go out of your way to support others. You never know when a little change that you make will lead to a big break. In my experience, opportunities never come at a time that matches my schedule. They never look the way I expect them to, either. I had to change what I was doing to get different results.

I have heard that we have an odd tendency to cling to activities that are familiar but do not advance our goals. If we can be flexible and make room in our lives for new habits, they will enrich us and move us towards the life of our dreams. Don't allow inconvenience to kill your dreams. This subtle and seductive thief prevents action when it is necessary. Seize the day and create room for the inconvenience tasks that make all the difference.

LIVE IN FAITH, NOT FEAR

In my experience, there are two ways to live your life—in fear or faith. I'm not talking about religious faith. What I mean by faith is a way of living your life where you focus your mind on the good and positive side of every outcome, and you ignore and discount any negative thoughts that are driven by fear.

Many people are living their lives based upon fear. They allow their thoughts to become negative and focus on what can go wrong, or what's bad in any situation. This may shrink their comfort zone due to fear of what others may think of them or that they might make a mistake. They do not go after their dreams due to the unknown that scares them or the potential of failure.

There are so many negative influences in our lives. The news is constantly providing negative reporting and new reasons to be scared of something. Commercials for products and especially political campaigns mostly prey on our fears. They want us to react to our fears and buy their product or vote for the less scary of two options. Fear is a dominant force in advertising.

Living in fear is very reactionary because this emotion causes us to bypass the normal thought processes of decision-making. In this way, our reactions are not fully considered or, sometimes, even rational. They are just driven by a fight or flight instinct. Advertisers and politicians have learned to manipulate people using this tactic.

When you live in faith, it means that you focus on the positive and expect an optimal outcome of any situation. You may still have fearful thoughts, but you choose not to allow them to control you. This means you don't make up stories in your mind about the bad things that can happen. Instead, you expect a positive result. If you make up stories in your mind, they will be about obtaining the best outcome in any situation.

When a negative thought or fear arises in my mind, I simply say to myself, "I choose to live in faith." Then I start to think about the best possible outcome. For example, I used to get nervous when I flew in an airplane. It seemed to come up the most just before take-off. My mind would begin to recall all the possible crash scenarios such as wind shears or engine failures. I would recall the news of the latest airline crash.

Then I started using the little trick of saying to myself, "I choose to live in faith." By doing this, I am choosing to expect that the take-off and flight will go just fine and that the slight chance of a problem isn't worth worrying. When I do this, I feel better immediately. My mind is calm, and I begin to think about the fun I'm going to have when I get there. It switches my thinking, and I relax.

It is pointless worrying about bad things. So why should I spend my time worrying about bad things when they rarely happen? This just makes me unhappy instead of enjoying the airplane ride. I enjoy the view from the window, and when I choose to live in faith, I change my focus to a positive outcome and reject my fears. It is a great way to take control of my mind when fears arise.

Let's consider the worst-case scenario. What if the plane crashed and I died? How would I want to go out? Would I want to go down in fear and dread or in a blissful state of enjoying my final descent expecting a safe landing? I would choose the latter. I would rather be a fool expecting to be saved up to my final moment, than a wretch that cannot see the bright side of anything. Which is the most fun way to live?

So living in faith has become my mantra when fears want to control me or cause a negative reaction. I choose to live in faith and you can too. Most fears are not rational, and people will use fear to manipulate if you allow it. So, recognize when you are in a state of fear and take positive action. You will live a much happier life in faith than anywhere else.

Meditation = Manifestation

As a novice, you learned about meditation walks. This is a great way to start the process of honoring yourself, gaining focus, and calming your mind. Another deeper way to meditate is in the lying or sitting position. There are various opinions on the best way to meditate, and you could spend years perfecting the practice. However, in my experience, it is not necessary to devote years of study to meditation to create positive results.

It is also not necessary to pretzel your body into a yoga position. Being flexible is great for your body and muscles, but is not a prerequisite for good meditation. Remember, you cannot do it wrong because there is no right or wrong way to do anything.

Just get into a comfortable position in a chair, lying on a bed or the floor, or sitting on the ground. The key is to be completely comfortable so that maintaining your body position will be a natural and effortless process. Some believe that overcoming discomfort is a part of meditation, but I disagree. I meditate in both the sitting and lying position often.

Guided meditation can be very helpful especially if meditation is new to you. There are many guided ones available on the Internet or through other sources. I like to wear headphones while I am doing a guided meditation since it cuts back on background noise and distractions. I recommend headphones that completely encircle your ears because ear buds and headphones that sit on top of the ears can become uncomfortable and don't provide as much noise-canceling. High-end headphones will be more likely to encircle your ears, but I have found inexpensive ones that do it as well.

There are guided meditations for health, wealth, relaxation, and many other things. I find the ones that are 30 minutes or less to be about the best length for me. Doing this type of meditation twice a day is more effective: once in the morning when I awake and once just before dinner. It calms my mind, recharges my energy, heals my body, focuses my thoughts, enhances creativity, and brings important tasks to mind. I always awaken feeling great.

During meditation, I sometimes repeat I AM statements or recite my mantra. I often imagine myself flying or traveling to beautiful places. I keep my thoughts positive and imagine the loving embrace of the universe and the good it wants for me. I also imagine the feeling of accomplishing my goals and celebrating the event with my friends.

When I'm in the zone of a meditative state, I can feel energy surging through my body and my nerve endings tingle with pleasure. A focused meditation provides a sensation that is better than any drug that nature or man has created. I feel as if I am floating or even flying. I feel the love and energy of the universe swirling in my mind and body.

In my experience, meditation is the process of manifestation. Consider this: personal development gurus all teach that you must imagine your future, feel worthy of it, focus on it, and raise your vibration to achieve your goals. By believing in yourself and becoming more, you will attract more to yourself. As Mike Dooley says, "Thoughts become things."

The process of mediation is precisely that. It allows you to get in touch with the feelings of success, enhances creativity, strengthens your personal belief, and focuses your mind on what you want. It builds your confidence, calms fears, and provides energy. It is manifestation in action.

Many times I have employed meditation for manifestation. While doing it, I focus on what I want and get in touch with the feeling of having it. I enter a state of peace and happiness that surges through my body. Afterward, I often find that an event or action has occurred that has brought my goal closer to me. It works like magic. I believe that meditation = manifestation, it is available to everyone, and it can be leveraged at any moment.

Once you experience this level of meditation, and see the results, you will look forward to it every day. It will become one of the most important parts of the process of taking care of yourself, getting what you want, and acknowledging the divine within.

CHAPTER SUMMARY

As a chosen one apprentice, you have come to believe that great success and wealth are possible for you. You have learned to become grateful for what you already have. You had the opportunity to decide what you want in your life regardless of previous self-imposed limitations. You are beginning to take action on your goals and use meditation for creativity and relaxation.

You began to look at your environment and make improvements to serve you better. You choose to rid yourself of anything that makes you feel bad. You realized that having the support of others is necessary to succeed and began to seek out like-minded friends. You learned to forgive others as a way to forgive yourself.

Proven strategies for success were discussed, and the simple process of conceive-believe-achieve was revealed. You discovered that excellence, mistakes, and inconvenience were necessary for advancement. Being outward focused and removing distractions were shown as important concepts.

Are you now ready to stretch your comfort zone and make mistakes? You will know you are ready to advance to the next level when you decide what you want, set goals to achieve it, define a higher purpose, believe it is possible for you, and accept that inconvenience is the price for success. Living in faith and not fear will become your mantra.

This is where the fun part of my life began. At this level, I was able to reconceive who I was and who I was capable of being and accomplishing. I decided to step away from my technical computer skills and move into online media and become an author. My technical skills had served me well, but I discovered they were not where my heart lies.

I set huge goals and started a radio station, became a podcast host, and author. I wanted to be a creator of my own

THE RISE OF THE CHOSEN ONES

intellectual property instead of an implementer of others. I wanted to teach others what I had learned and become a thought leader for a better world.

Deciding what I wanted was not the daunting task I had always imagined. It was inside of me all the time waiting for me to believe it was possible. It is still evolving as well. In alignment with my vision, I am still finding new ways to revolutionize media in a positive way. My clear intention is always finding new mechanisms for manifestation.

As a review, here are steps the apprentice needs to accomplish.

1. Self-value, self-concept, I am concept
2. Believe it is possible for you
3. Stretch comfort zone
4. Become grateful
5. Forgive others
6. Conceive-Believe-Achieve
7. Decide what you want
8. Transform Your Environment
9. Encourage mistakes
10. Intellectual property is key
11. Decide to be inconvenienced
12. Live in faith not fear
13. Meditation = manifestation

11

~~~

JOURNEYMAN

THE JOURNEYMAN

*The purpose of the journeyman level is to put your
goals into action, believe they are possible, and
overcome the fears that stand in your way.*

The fourth chosen one attainment level is about belief
and becoming action oriented. Confidence is gained
by doing and showing commitment and persistence.
Here you will take action steps towards your goals and begin
to overcome the fear walls. You will learn to use strategies,
have fun, and persistence will be developed by staying in
motion. Making steady progress towards your goals is the
journeyman stage.

You will take advantage of many proven success strategies
such as intellectual property, win-win, leverage, distraction
management, and seeking excellence, not perfection. You will

connect with infinite intelligence. You will seek out and join forces with others who are on the same path.

What will emerge is a rock solid, positive belief system about yourself and your abilities. You will use the tools of responsibility, overcoming fears, negotiation, and accomplishment to fuel your future and passion. The magic of transformation in your life is about to happen.

Trust the process and take the risks that are necessary to keep moving. Always take the next step and don't worry about the outcome. You cannot foresee the wonders that will result from unwavering progress.

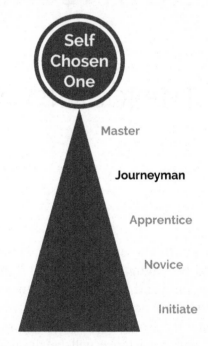

OVERCOME FEAR WALLS

At this level, Fear is the dream killer. It can prevent you from taking action and constrict your life back to mediocrity. Do not allow this to happen. Fear comes in many forms. For example, there are natural fears such as pain and death. However, many unnatural fears are only in the mind and not real.

They are imagined fears, such as failure, success, fame, small places, heights, and countless other invented phobias. Natural fears are rational and are in place to protect the body. Imagined fears are overcome by changing one's thought patterns, taking action, and practice.

To expand our comfort zone, our fears need to be challenged. Fears left to fester in the mind will grow larger and reduce the size of our comfort zone. When we consistently push against these fears, it expands our limiting beliefs. Limiting beliefs are fear based, so once we reduce fears, our beliefs will expand and so will our capabilities.

In my experience, fears are often assembled in layers. Pushing through a lower layer leaves the outer layers still in place. I call these fear walls. As we take action towards our goals, a fear wall will rise in some area such as exercise. When we start to exercise, we may fear the pain of sore muscles or even having a heart attack. However, once we push through the initial fear wall to start the process, all fear of exercise does not go away.

There may be a fear wall that running a mile is impossible. There may be another fear wall of how much weight we can lose. The list goes on. We must repeatedly break through these fear walls to expand our level of exercise and improve our health. Each time we do this, our overall level of fear goes down, and we get better at overcoming our fears.

Persistence Development

If there is a characteristic that trumps all others, it is persistence. If you have this, then everything you do will work, and without it, nothing you do will work. Persistence is the difference between success and failure in all cases. Persistence is never giving up and continuing to take action even in the face of failure or mistakes.

Consider Thomas Edison and the light bulb. He tried more than 1,000 different ways to make it work. His detractors finally came to him and asked him when he was going to give up. He replied by saying that he had already discovered almost all the ways that it would not work and knew he was very close to the solution. That is a great example of persistence.

There are a couple of other concepts that are closely related to persistence. They are intention and self-discipline. Self-discipline is the ability to make yourself do something even when you don't feel like it. Intention is the dedication to an outcome that transcends any single solution. When I speak of persistence, I include these meanings as well.

To me, being persistent is having a goal that you will never give up. A goal that you are willing to attempt any solution to achieve, and one that may require you to do things you don't feel like doing. That is persistence as I have defined it here.

In my career as a computer network engineer and software programmer, I have often been able to leverage persistence. Many times I have run into weird computer, network, and software issues that are stubborn to isolate, track down, and fix. Then, even when I think the problem is solved it can recur. In certain cases, it can take weeks and months to find the solution. The only thing that works is persistence by constantly employing new techniques and strategies.

As an example, I was working for a cable TV company in Seattle and in charge of a new software application that produced printed work orders. At one location, the printer that produced the work orders would always add odd characters that caused constant reprinting. My boss put me in charge of fixing this.

I spent weeks driving to this location, swapping out equipment, making software changes, and working with the vendor to fix the problem, but nothing worked. I was frustrated and eventually called in help from our cable TV engineers. They, too, were stumped. You know a problem is tough when everyone including the vendor is stumped.

Nevertheless, I kept going there every morning and printing the work orders myself to figure it out. Finally, one of the cable engineers had an idea. He noticed that the printer was located right next to the cable TV "head end" room. There were hundreds of devices in there that produced radio transmissions at different frequencies.

We decided to run a ground wire from the building to a bolt on the chassis of the printer as a test. As soon as this was in place, the printer behaved perfectly. It had been picking up the odd characters wirelessly from the room next door. The problem finally was solved after weeks of effort.

Persistence means you leverage your team as necessary. In this case, my fellow technical staff, because success and goal seeking are a team sport. If you do not have a team, then you must enroll others to help you. Their opinions and ideas will fill in the blind spots in your strategies. Their encouragement will carry you through when you are discouraged.

I suggest you choose your team wisely and make sure it is filled with those who know how to focus on the positive. Even people with great talent cannot be allowed on your team if they complain and do not know how to support others. The hit to morale and persistence will be too high. So find positive people to support you.

Another idea is to find a place in your life where you already exhibit persistence. It could be at your job, in your relationships, with your children, or your devotion to your health. We all have life areas where we show this. It is how we get things done, so find yours.

Then, transfer that high level of persistence to your goals and dreams. Just apply that same standard to a new area of your life, and raise your standards instead of allowing yourself to be mediocre. The truth is you cannot fail when you never give up, so be persistent above all else.

ACT WITH RESPONSIBILITY

Previously, we discussed responsibility and how when we operate with responsibility, we accept the consequences of our actions, even if they are not what we intended. We learned that blaming others for our lives gets in the way of learning and growth. This also includes the way we communicate with others.

Marshall Thurber's definition of communication is, "the response I get." This means that if someone else doesn't understand what you said or got a different message, then you didn't communicate it well enough. In other words, they didn't get it. Therefore, you take responsibility for being unclear and find another way to help them understand. You may also take the time to have them repeat what you said to make sure they got it.

Living a life without blame means that you take responsibility when things go wrong. You want to learn and be better so always ask yourself, "What can I learn from this situation?" This keeps you on the learning team, so you don't have to be perfect. You just need to pay attention to your mistakes and make changes to be better.

Being responsible for your life also feels good. You feel stronger in any situation where you exercise responsibility and refuse to be a victim. You will become more than you once were, and will be rewarded at a higher level.

Progress Towards Vision

The journeyman by definition is actively making progress towards their goals. They are utilizing all the concepts in the dynamics model to bring their goals into reality. This is truly the action stage of the process. Creative ideas are flowing from meditation and you, the chosen ones, are now operating on faith that the universe will provide whatever is needed at the right moment.

The proven strategies that have a highly predictable outcome are now being employed, and you are building a winning team for success. You are making focused time each day to work on your goals and foster your personal beliefs. Commitment and persistence are the characteristics on which you must rely. Faith and trust in yourself and your vision are now your way of life. You are humble enough to ask for help and enrolling others in your cause who are inspired by your higher purpose.

At this point, the results of your personal development work begin to appear. The time and preparation work begins to bear fruit. You are moving forward and taking risks, and the outcome is not important; the creative process and belief are what drives you to stay in motion.

As a writer, you have decided on your book concept, and you're adding pages on a consistent basis. As an artist, you have picked a medium and are taking the time to create daily. As a businessperson, you have mastered a skill and are marketing your product or services. You are building new relationships and meeting new people. Your health and well-being are attended to each day.

The setbacks and negative opinions of others that once crushed your dreams are now just feedback on how to improve your services. You disregard the meaningless comments of those without vision. You recognize that most others have no goals and will resent those who do. Those that complain are not doers and are not happy with themselves. Therefore, you do not waste time your time and energy with those that do not understand.

Your self-concept is now built up to the point where you trust your instincts and ideas. Original ideas are flowing towards you easily and effortlessly. Your actions are resulting in accomplishments and contacts that you have never had before. You are amazed at what you are capable of doing. You can call anyone and ask for what you want. Each day you are taking bigger risks and setting even higher goals as you grow and expand.

You say yes to new opportunities even if you have never done them before. You live in the world of "and" so you do not limit yourself to just a few projects. You know you can do this, that, and something else at the same time. Your productive capacity keeps growing. Your creativity takes you in many directions, and you explore them and keep doing what works. Your productivity and resourcefulness have risen to unprecedented levels.

When a method is no longer serving its purpose, you drop it and take up something new or concentrate on the others that are paying dividends. You are finding new interests and are no longer defined by what you did in the past. Your future is once again exciting and bright.

〜〜〜

INTERACT WITH OTHERS ON THE PATH

There is strength in numbers, and no one should ever need to travel the path to greatness alone. In fact, many groups support and encourage those who want more out of their lives. The Internet has made it easy to meet people around the world and make connections that will enhance your personal and professional life.

You can start simple and join a social group that has an interest in personal development, wealth, or manifestation. The Meetup.com website has many of these groups. There are Abraham-Hicks Law of Attraction groups throughout the United States that meet regularly. Almost everyone who attends these groups will have a positive mindset and can help encourage progress. It is a great way to meet new friends.

A way to take things up another level is to seek out or create a mastermind group. Mastermind groups work together to accomplish projects and pool the resources of the group to get things done. The group will typically focus on a goal and then put together a plan to accomplish it. All members of the group work together, they do the research and provide resources and labor.

After I graduated from college, I put together a mastermind group to focus on business opportunities. I enrolled two of my friends, and we met every two weeks and discussed potential opportunities. Once we selected a target opportunity, we each researched a part of it to determine if it warranted further exploration.

We explored website hosting, website design, automobile sales, and real estate investing. Eventually, we chose real estate investing and began to learn about the process. After a few meetings and reading books such as *Rich Dad, Poor Dad*, we began to make some investments. One from the group focused on apartment buildings while I focused on single-family homes. It was a great success, and I still have investments because of this group.

Another way to help build your support team is to take classes on topics that you want to learn. Many focus on specific knowledge such as real estate, stocks, bonds, options, and online marketing. These are excellent ways to gain knowledge where needed. For some people, this is all that is required.

However, for many, these classes will not be effective because what they need is not knowledge; it is confidence, belief, and a sense of purpose. Without these critical concepts, you will never be able to take consistent action on your goals. This is why personal development courses deliver far better results than knowledge classes.

When you have a sense of purpose and high self-concept, everything you do and learn can be put into immediate action. Without these concepts, you always will find difficulty with any business project because you will be standing in your own way. Quite simply, with a high self-concept everything works, without it, nothing works.

PSI Seminars has a great set of basic and advanced courses that can make everything you do more successful because they help clear away what is holding you back. All the knowledge you have been gathering your whole life can finally be put to good use. PSI Seminars also has a community you can join. The concepts take some time to learn so, in the meantime, mingle with a group that is having success.

My wife and I attend an annual meeting in California and have learned from some of the greatest minds of our time including Bob Proctor, Mike Dooley, Wayne Dyer, Brian Tracy, Marshall Thurber, and many more. Staying involved in a like-minded group keeps us focused on moving forward and achieving our dreams.

APPLY WIN-WIN

Win-win is one of four possible negotiation strategies. A win-win solution allows both parties to get what they want. It is important to think this way and apply it to your life as a journeyman. The most successful people and companies are always looking for win-win solutions. Once you master this technique, you will always be in-demand as a partner for any new project or venture.

My stepfather was a very successful lawyer in the Seattle area. He did the legal work for the upscale Bellevue Town Square Mall among other projects. He once told me the reason he was so successful in real estate negotiation was that he always took the time to find out what the other party wanted. Once he knew this, he could structure the deal, so they both won. He became highly sought after for big real estate deals due to his ability to find mutually agreeable solutions.

I also consider my agreement with Jim Britt, who was Tony Robbins's first mentor as a win-win example. I was building my Internet Radio Station called Program Your Life Radio. I needed compelling audio content to put on the station, and I had no revenues to offer for compensation. A friend of mine suggested that I contact Jim because we may have similar goals. So, I obtained his phone number and asked for ten minutes of his time.

I told him about my station and how I wanted to transform the radio media to make it more positive and inspirational. He listened, and after I had finished talking, he asked what he could do to help. Then I offered to help promote his products and services using my websites, radio station, and social networks. In exchange, I needed broadcast rights to audio content, which I knew he had.

I also asked him if there were any particular causes that he was interested in, and how I might be able to help. He told me about his wife's campaign to end human trafficking called Good Women International. I agreed to help any way I could, starting with writing blog posts about the issue. For more information about this topic go to http://www.goodwomen. org/

The result of our conversations was a deal that allowed the radio station to broadcast his complete audio series called *The Power of Letting Go*. In exchange, my station runs public service announcements, advertises his products, and promotes Good Women International. There is no financial compensation required by either side.

My radio station obtained hours of compelling audio content; he received additional marketing for his products, and his wife's campaign to end human trafficking obtained a publicity partner. We both got what we wanted in this win-win deal.

Jim Britt has several audio programs and is an excellent motivational speaker. If you wish to know more about him, I urge you to visit his website at http://www.jimbritt.com.

APPLY LEVERAGE OF ALL TYPES

Suppose your dream is to market and deliver products or services, and you don't want to do it all by yourself. This is a great idea because involving others in your business is a form of leverage. Some make the mistake of thinking they can do it alone. They may start personal service businesses such as massage therapy or personal consulting that have low leverage. Since you only have two hands to work with and 24 hours in a day, your income is limited in a personal services business.

However, if you employ some sort of leverage instead, the upside becomes unlimited. Leverage is a business concept that many first time entrepreneurs overlook. Leverage comes in many forms: financial, social, network, and capital to name a few. For a business to have the greatest success make sure it has lots of leverage potential.

One of the best ways to utilize leverage in the 21st century is to use the Internet. The Internet is the best leverage vehicle ever invented. A single website or blog post can potentially be viewed by millions or even billions of customers. The Internet can be used for marketing your product and even delivering it when providing information or digital content. Marshall Thurber, a master business teacher, and visionary believes it is a good idea to use the Internet as a part of your leverage strategy.

Marshall Thurber has mentored many successful people such as Robert Kiyosaki, Jack Canfield, and Tony Robbins to name a few. He is regarded as the teacher of teachers when it comes to personal and business success. According to Marshall, "Network Science is the predominant dynamic for success in the 21st Century". One of his students, Robert Kiyosaki, is the best-selling author of the *Rich Dad, Poor Dad* book series, and workshops. Robert is an expert on real estate investing and leverage. Robert says, "The rich build networks, the poor look for work."

This means that everyone who is serious about getting out of the rat race should be in the network business. The power of networks has made thousands of people rich through the leverage they provide. Let's explore the concept of network science. Network science explains how most social networks operate.

The basic building block of a social network is a node. Each person in the network is considered a node, and when two nodes become connected they form a link. A group of nodes linked together is called a cluster. Clusters are formed by preferential attachment. This means that the nodes choose to be linked such as when they become friends on Facebook or follow each other on Twitter. A very large cluster is called a hub. See the diagram below for a visual diagram.

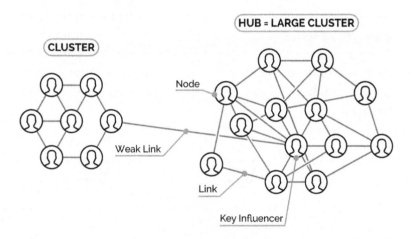

Each cluster or hub of nodes (people) is connected to all the others through what is called a weak link. Weak links are when someone from one cluster is connected to a person in another cluster. This is how two different circles of friends are connected. Weak links can be used to navigate the network and connect to any node you wish. According to Marshall Thurber, we are only 5.5 degrees of separation from every other person on the planet leveraging network science. So using it you can reach anyone you want.

Each social network has a few very large hubs at its center, and these hubs dominate the network due to their size and influence. Therefore, if you want to control any network, the key is to control the top five hubs within it. This can be done by finding the key influencers within the hubs and making them a part of your network. Key influencers can be identified because they have more links than other nodes.

Once one of the key influencers of a hub is identified, they can be leveraged to control the entire hub. The next step is to move to the next major hub and do it again. This can be done using trusted weak links. These weak links can assist with introductions into the next hub.

Social networks do not have normal population distribution curves because the data is not random. Instead, they have a series of clusters and hubs that range from small to large that create the network power curve. The large hubs at the top of the curve have the most power. If you can control the top five hubs of any network, you effectively control the network.

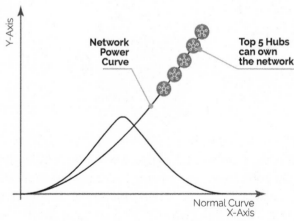

Leverage is the key ingredient to the success that networks provide. What exactly is Leverage? Leverage comes from the simple concept of a lever which was invented in ancient times to help move large objects with a long pole and a fulcrum. The amount of pressure that was needed to move objects was much smaller when applied at the end of a long pole or lever. One man could multiply his strength by many times through the use of a lever. That same concept of multiplying your efforts through leverage still applies today, and it can be exercised in modern times through the use of networks.

Examples of leverage through networks today are everywhere. Authors use books for leverage because they write them once and can sell them many times. Actors make movies that are shown to millions. Television and Radio networks broadcast a single show or song to many thousands of listeners. Professional athletes exercise leverage through the media coverage they acquire by being top performers. Banks use leverage by making loans that require small financial reserves.

How can the average personal looking for success use leverage? One way to easily create your own leverage is by creating a network or getting into alignment with an existing network. There are lots of ways to do this. Let's look at getting into alignment with an existing network. This involves less effort than creating your own. The process involves two basic steps: first, join an existing business network; second, develop the skills and belief in yourself to build your team within this network.

These existing networks also provide you with the support needed to be successful. They provide training, knowledge, motivation, and technical resources. Some have online websites to recruit customers and clients who will help you build your business. In summary, you must learn to leverage a network if you want to be successful in the 21st century.

As I mentioned previously, Robert Kiyosaki is well known for his *Rich Dad, Poor Dad* series of books and seminars. In his books, he talks about his friend's father who becomes his rich dad. Few people actually know this, but the character-rich dad was inspired by a great teacher. He was not entirely made up by Robert as some people believe. There is a lot of confusion around this.

The inspiration for Rich Dad is still around, and he continues to teach thousands every year ways to become a success in business and life. In fact, you can still take a seminar from him if you act quickly. His team has created several outstanding courses, and they start with a three-day workshop called Business and You. The great teacher's name is Marshall Thurber, and his guidance and mentorship have changed my life and many others. For more information about his courses see this website: http://burklynglobal.com/courses/.

MAKE MISTAKES AND LEARN

As a journeyman, it is time to break down your goals into action plans and put tasks into action. Based upon your actions, you'll start receiving the necessary feedback to refine your approach. Mistakes you make will provide the feedback needed to learn, they are inevitable and required. Do not wait until you are better prepared to get started. Planning can only take you so far because nothing goes as planned.

Now is the time to start that business, file for the licenses, trademark your logos, and select those business cards. Put up your website even if it is only your contact information. You can improve it later as you learn what your customers want. Start writing your book, play, or screenplay. Hire your physical trainer and lose the weight. Make a list of your action steps and keep track of your progress.

Begin marketing your product or service and see how it is received. If buyers are not beating your door down, then find out from them what you can do to make your product more compelling. Potential as well as existing customers are your best source of information, and they usually are happy to provide feedback. Make changes immediately when you receive valuable feedback.

Some people say you never get a second chance to make a first impression. Perhaps this is true, but you have to risk making a bad impression to figure out what they like, and a bad impression is better than no impression. Besides, there are plenty of potential customers, so do not worry about losing a few during the startup process.

Many of them will come back to you once they discover you have made changes to serve them. The customers are not rejecting you; they are just rejecting the deal because it is not yet compelling enough. Every time you don't get a sale, ask them what you can do next time to make it more compelling. They will appreciate that you care enough to ask their opinion.

Mistakes must be made to succeed. The most successful people are better at making mistakes. They make more of them faster and react quicker. So use every mistake as a learning experience, and you will be on the fast track to success in any field.

INTELLECTUAL PROPERTY DEVELOPMENT

Now is the time to develop your intellectual property. This is the key to your future success because you will control something that nobody else has. Intellectual property (IP) is the key to almost all successful businesses and is highly protected by the laws of most western countries. To do this, you can create your own IP or purchase the right to use someone else's. I recommend creating your own.

IP is so simple to create. It can be music, video, books, poems, a course curriculum, even business or technical processes. It can be an invention, software, a website, online service, mobile application, game, product, a unique service, or artwork. The market is hungry for the next great idea in the form of IP and is willing to pay dearly.

The journeyman is actively in the process of creation. They are creating and then marketing their IP. Your objective is to create as many products and services as possible that, with the help of others, you can market. You can create the IP on your own, but will need others to market, finance and distribute it successfully.

So, plan to give away part of the ownership and profits because sharing is having more. A percentage of a shared big company is better than 100% of a small company.

You do not need a Ph.D., technical certifications, or even a college degree to create IP. Most IP is a simple idea or an improvement to an existing product or service. I'm sure, over your lifetime, you have had many of these ideas.

Now is the time to document the details, start the process of creating them, and share your ideas with your mentors and coaches. They will help you with the creation process and find the connections needed to birth the ideas.

IP creates dynamic value, and it can be leveraged into great wealth and even fame. You must have it to become a master chosen one. So focus on what you love and create new IP in that area. It will become the master key to your success.

DISTRACTION MANAGEMENT

We pay a high price when we allow distractions to control our time and take away our focus; the action-oriented journeyman needs to manage their distractions and remove them wherever possible. Some tough choices occasionally have to be made on how we use our time and how many leisure activities we can allow ourselves. Sometimes this is the price we must pay for greater freedom and personal liberty.

Fortunately, there are techniques we can use to manage distractions and use our time more efficiently. Many time management books give in-depth techniques on this subject. We can master distractions in several ways; here are just a few ideas to get you started.

The first way is by protecting your most productive hours of the day. Early morning until about noon is when we can focus on tasks and activities at our highest level. We must be protective of this time by shifting activities that don't require a high degree of focus to later in the day.

Email is a prime example if you work in an office. In the past, the first thing I did each morning was sort through unread email. This process could take a couple of hours, could lead to several other various tasks, and by the time the process was finished my mornings were mostly over. I counteracted this by shifting email to just before lunch, and I reserved my mornings for important projects and tasks when my mind was fresher, and I was able to complete more tasks.

A second way to remove distractions is to stop doing things that fill your time and produce few results. Watching TV at night is a prime example. This can consume many productive hours each week, and the negative effects of most TV shows will degrade your attitude. TV shows have become violent, greed based, and most characters are terrible role models. There are exceptions to this but spending lots of time in front of the TV will almost guarantee your goals will not be achieved. This time could be better spent focusing on your goals, accomplishing tasks, making contacts and performing critical thinking.

A third way to manage your time is to keep a list of your tasks and start every morning by going over the list. Then, choose at least one item that you will accomplish on that day. If your tasks are too big to accomplish in just one day, then break them down into smaller units until you can. It's important that you scratch at least one item off the list each day, as it will keep you in motion towards your goals.

SEEK EXCELLENCE

The journeyman seeks excellence, which means making constant improvements towards the standard of excellence, and not perfection. This does not mean that you need to start at excellence, sometimes you may not even be proud of where you start, but making the start is the most important thing. Most products and services are not initially delivered with excellence because it takes time and practice to achieve, so do not wait for it.

Anything worth doing is worth doing badly for a while until you figure it out. Whether it is exercise, spirituality, or a product or service, everything has a humble beginning. No matter how old you are, a beginner's mind is required to learn new things. So embrace the learning process and improve as you go. Excellence is the long-term goal not the standard to get started.

There are many examples of successful people and businesses that began awkwardly and had to redefine themselves through the improvement process. For example, Yamaha began as a piano company and IBM started by making typewriters. It is by making mistakes that we receive the information necessary to adapt and get better. This helps us refine the creative process and gives new ideas and opportunities.

We strive for excellence in our lives and our activities; however, it should never be used as an excuse for not taking action. Excellence comes from repetition and practice at new things. It is not the starting position. Happily learning new things is what makes life exciting and fresh. So for best results, take action first and seek excellence along the way. Your life will be much fuller and more surprising.

～≫～

HAVE FUN AND ENJOY THE JOURNEY

A wise friend and counselor I know named Rita Soman once told me if your inner child doesn't get excited about your goals, neither will you. She said, "Your inner child is always with you, no matter how old you are. It gets excited the way a five-year-old does about our lives. It wants to have fun and play." Therefore, if you are having problems achieving your dreams, perhaps it is because your inner child just isn't into it.

Maybe your goals are just too boring, or perhaps they involve helping other people and not you. Do you have a goal to support others? Do you want to change the world? Do you want social change? Do you want justice? These are all noble goals and things that are lacking in the world. However, your inner child may be saying, what's in it for me?

It wants to know how it will benefit and how much fun it will have doing it. It won't be excited about helping others until its needs are met. So ask yourself, are my goals going to take care of me first, so that I can help others from a place of abundance? Also, are my goals going to be fun in the future and along the journey? Perhaps they are just too serious or lacking in self-benefits.

I have made this mistake myself. When I was younger, I focused on very adult oriented things such as financial independence, building a business, accomplishing tasks, and education. I made good progress initially but would run out of energy and end up exhausted. There were too many HAD TO do's in my goals, but not many WANT TO do's.

Face it, nothing you have to do is fun. That is why it is called work. Work involves a thing we don't like to do, and it takes away our energy. Anything that takes away energy is not sustainable over the long run. Also, my inner child was bored out of his mind. He was not having fun and would constantly distract me. I would waste time watching TV and playing video games to appease him.

Rita told me your inner child wants to play and have fun. Whatever you do make sure there is an element of fun in it. Otherwise, your goals will be something you have to do instead of something you want to do. Doing what you want provides energy. Also, she suggested not creating a goal of helping others unless it also involved helping me. She said, "Your inner child will be excited when they benefit from it, and they will provide more energy for your dreams."

What she means is we get excited about our lives when our goals have self-benefit, and we are having fun along the journey towards them. So if your goals don't include some fun then figure out a way to add it, or perhaps choose a goal that is more fun. I learned this lesson when I was creating my Internet radio station called Program Your Life Radio.

The station is about personal growth and development. I had big name speakers such as Bob Proctor on the station, and I had good music and meditations between shows. However, when I looked closely at it, I was making a station for those who took their personal improvement seriously.

Then I thought, where is the fun? Shouldn't it be fun, too? Therefore, I changed my slogan to "We Make Personal Growth Fun." Next, I found a comedy show to spice things up, plus some edgy musicians to energize the music. More recently, I added Andy Dooley to the station. Andy has a wacky, humorous style that makes all his content easy to learn and a terrific, fun ride. This has made everything more fun.

So make sure that everything you do and every goal you make has fun in it. This makes the process a great time and adds energy and motivation. I suggest you check in with your inner child to make sure they are excited about the goals you set. They will guide you along the way and provide you with joy and happiness. If you make your goals fun, you will never have to work again.

For more information about Rita Soman or PSYCH-K go to http://ritasoman.com/.

OVERCOME STORY MAKING

Here is a fact: we all make up stories about the meaning of our world, others' thoughts, and our self-worth. These stories are how we perceive the world. We must be aware of this story making and observe when it is negative, and it can be very negative if we lack faith in our abilities. Once we identify negative story making, we can stop it and change the process. We can interrupt the inner dialog in our heads and laugh at the absurdity of it.

Two simple ways to overcome this process include being aware of it and redirecting our focus. We can learn to monitor and control our minds and become selective of the thoughts we allow. Here are some easy solutions to help manage story making.

The first solution is not to engage in story making. It's not a hard process to change; it's just two easy steps. First, become aware of when you find yourself making up a story or dialog about an upcoming meeting or event. This is when we imagine the future event and decide how it might go. You may find your mind wandering and may even begin to engage in a fake conversation about some issue that has arisen. You may decide if my spouse says this again I'm going to let her know how I feel about it this time, and if she reacts that way, I will say this, too. This type of story making happens easily and often, and we need to become aware of it because these stories are not real.

So now you have become aware of it, next, stop yourself from doing this. Once you realize you're in story making mode, halt the mental process. One technique is to laugh at yourself and think about how funny it is that you do this. Sometimes I say to myself. "That's a great story, thanks for sharing." On the other hand, I will think, "I sure can make up some good stories." It's very amusing to see how quickly I make stuff up and the wild conversations I invent.

Another idea is to change the fake negative story to a better one. Think of the best possible story you could make up about the outcome, instead of a bad one. After all, if you are going to make stuff up it should be fun and helpful, not hurtful and holding you back. For example, don't imagine a negative outcome from someone saying "We need to talk." Imagine instead that they just want to spend quality time with you and tell you how much they appreciate all the little things you do. Shift your stories to the positive, and you will become energized and excited about your life.

We can change that inner dialog to a positive one. We can think about how an event could work out great for us instead of against us. This positive approach changes our feelings from fear to faith, reduces stress, and once we are in a positive mind space, we can take actions that will benefit others and ourselves.

CONNECT WITH INFINITE INTELLIGENCE

The universe has a mysterious intelligence that both defines scientific laws and guides future events and outcomes. As much as we attempt to control our lives and environment, we find unknown forces often befuddle our efforts. As Buckminster Fuller wrote, "When we consider this, we ultimately reach the conclusion that we are not running this world."

However, even though we are not in charge of the world, we can comprehend and harness the immutable laws. When we work in harmony with these laws, positive outcomes are guaranteed. When we work against them or believe we are in control, the result is struggle and stress. In my experience, it is not necessary for us to be in control of our lives, we just need to trust that the universe has a positive plan for us.

In the moments of your life when you perceive that feeling of love for yourself or another, you are in alignment with infinite intelligence. The universe is always working towards a positive outcome for you, but it may not look like what you expect. When we connect with infinite intelligence, we disconnect from the outcome but make our desires known. Based on our desires, the universe always knows the best way to make it happen.

Follow that feeling of love, and you will be guided. The universe will then bring into your life people and events that are necessary for you to stay in alignment with what you love. When you show love for others, you are also showing love for yourself because we are all connected. Just as we are connected to infinite intelligence, we are also connected to each other. We live in a fully integrated social web. Everything we do affects all of us together, and you are never separated from the universal consciousness.

Understanding that you are continuously connected with infinite intelligence and others means that all your actions matter. Every positive action improves the world, and every negative action tears it apart. Every positive thought enhances your life, and every kindness you show makes the world kinder. Now it is your turn to make your mark in the world; how will you lead us?

FEEL THE FEELING OF GOALS ACHIEVED

We already know that feelings of success come before goal achievement. We get a sense of delight when the goal draws near, and this may even drive the final manifestation of the goal. Andy Dooley, the author of *Vibration Activation*, is convinced of this. He says the process for goal achievement is feeling first and manifestation second. I agree with Andy that the best way to manifest your goals quickly is to spend time imagining the result you want and feel the feeling of achievement in advance.

It is easy to do and can be done during meditation, while taking a walk, or in a couple of minutes of alone time each day. I suggest in the morning for maximum benefit. Feel the feeling of accomplishing your goals and expect great things to happen each day. I have done this for years, and whenever I do, good things happen.

To do this, I will go into a meditation and imagine the goal or dream I want to achieve and begin to feel those positive feelings. I will spend 10-15 minutes doing this and invariably afterward I will discover that some great thing happened while I was in this state. It is like magic! The feelings seem to bring about the outcome.

Begin to use this in your life and prove it to yourself. Imagine the outcome, feel the feeling, and good things will happen for you as long as you are in motion towards your goal. If you are action oriented and stay in touch with the feeling of success, it will happen.

CHAPTER SUMMARY

In this chapter, we focused on the value of taking action and the benefits that arise from staying in motion towards your goals. We started by focusing on overcoming the beliefs that cause fear, limit ourselves, and constrict the comfort zone. The values of persistence and responsibility were discussed.

You learned to make daily progress towards your vision, with an emphasis on acting with responsibility. The journeyman always is acting to build their team and find other positive minded people with whom to interact. Proven strategies such as intellectual property and leverage were revealed so that your efforts will have maximum results.

Effective habits are developed at this level. Habits of distraction management, excellence, having fun, and overcoming negative story making are put to the test. You are learning to live your future right now. Having a good connection with infinite intelligence will pull you through when things don't go as planned. The sustained efforts required for success are supported by meditation, faith development, and that wonderful feeling of goal achievement. If you never quit, you are unstoppable.

You will know you are ready to advance to the next level once your goals, based on a higher purpose, have been made a reality. To accomplish this, you will have surrounded yourself with a team that supports the vision. You will have created powerful intellectual property and learned to leverage it. Taking action will have become a way of life, and you will be looking for new challenges.

This is my current attainment level although I have mastered many of the concepts. My vision to revolutionize media in a positive way is still underway, and my focus is taking action towards its accomplishment. Every day I am further developing my habits so that action is always being taken.

I use daily meditations for creativity, belief development, and clarity of thought. I am always studying my craft to become better. I attend interactive personal development courses several times a year to better understand who I am. I look for ways to be uncomfortable and grow. I am grateful for my challenges and would rather have them than be bored by life.

My daily habits and challenges are to avoid distractions and keep my focus on what I want. I am always asking myself, what else do I need to learn to be better? And, how can I be of more service to the world? I keep my awareness on the stories I am making up in my mind. Are they serving me? As I learn and grow both emotionally and mentally, I keep my intention on becoming a master by manifesting my vision and enjoying the ride.

As a review, the steps of the journeyman as listed below.

1. Overcome fear walls
2. Persistence development
3. Act with responsibility
4. Progress towards vision
5. Interact with others on the path
6. Apply Win-Win
7. Apply leverage of all types
8. Make mistakes and learn
9. Intellectual property development
10. Distraction management
11. Seek excellence
12. Have fun and enjoy the journey
13. Overcome story making
14. Connect with infinite intelligence
15. Feel the feeling of goals achieved

12

~~~

MASTER

THE MASTER

The purpose of the master level is to achieve your visions with gratitude, humility, and to teach others the process.

The attainment of the master level is the ultimate goal. These chosen ones have successfully developed and implemented personal systems to overcome distractions, the comfort zone, others' opinions, and negative thoughts. Their health, relationships, clarity of thought, self-love, forgiveness, and sense of responsibility are functioning at high levels.

They have achieved supreme persistence, find joy in everything, and live for the moment. They have willed their dreams into reality through taking action and enrolling others. They understand how to take a vision and oversee a persistent process until it is achieved. They have accomplished the vision for their lives and this vision is now helping enrich the lives of others.

They live for a higher purpose and are guided by faith, intuition, and gratefulness. They are very selective of their friends, influences, and their personal environment. They have a supreme belief in themselves and can accomplish any task they choose. They find happiness and joy in everything they do, and they do not participate in activities that are not fulfilling.

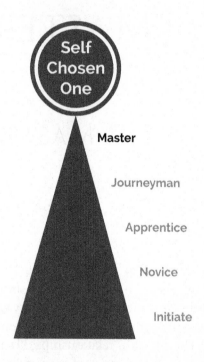

Following the path, they became a master in one or two areas of life and then sought to master all of them. They enjoy the constant challenge of self-growth and self-mastery. They have a deep love for themselves, other people, and for all of humanity. They are guided by a higher purpose, their faith, and take total responsibility for all outcomes, both good and bad. They know that everything is perfect in life no matter how it seems at first glance.

Masters have become more interested in creating success for others than for themselves. They actively seek to teach and mentor so that all can enjoy the abundance of the world. They wish to pass on the wisdom they have learned to the next generation and beyond. As we begin to discuss the master attainment level, let us return to the key concept of belief.

HIGH SELF-VALUE AND SELF-CONCEPT

As a master, your self-concept has developed to a high point. You now know you are worthy of anything you choose. When there are critical tasks to be done you know, you are the best person to lead the effort. Your accomplishments make you the person others seek out for advice.

You consider yourself a key player in any endeavor. You always take a leading role in any project, or you are not interested in being involved. You know that you are capable of anything, even if you haven't done it previously. You have the self-discipline to command yourself to take action and then follow through.

You have high personal standards for yourself and others. You expect excellence in everything you do and do not compromise on quality. You enjoy exceeding others' expectations, and you would never be involved in any company or project that goes against your values or that under delivers.

You expect others to treat you with respect just as you would treat them. You treat all people kindly and are humble. You are interested in other life stories and enjoy learning new skills and exploring ideas. You give credit to your team and support the development of their skills and abilities. You are always helping to create new leaders.

∽∾

INDIFFERENCE TO OTHERS OPINIONS

At the lower attainment levels, the negative opinions of others can influence us. In fact, we may use their perceptions as a way to justify what we are doing, because we need the validation. We can crave and encourage others to say nice things about us, often called "fishing for a compliment." However, by the time you have become a master, this is no longer the case.

You know you have reached the master level when you are no longer concerned with what others think or say about you. You recognize that your opinion is the only one that truly matters. This is not to say you no longer invite feedback. You still enjoy receiving feedback to improve yourself and your projects. You just reach your own conclusions as to what it means.

As a master, you now have a committed team and inner circle of trusted friends to act as confidants. You highly prize their counsel and advice, although you trust your instincts and wisdom to make final decisions. Once a choice is made, you take action and move forward with courage and persistence. You are also unafraid to change course if the situation changes or a mistake is identified.

You do not seek out or pay attention to those who criticize you or your projects. You take your feedback from the natural environment, your process controls, and your advisors. Professional critics have little to contribute, so you avoid exposing yourself to negativity.

GRATEFUL FOR EVERYTHING

Would you like to be grateful for all the fortunes and struggles in your life? To be grateful for all the vicissitudes that some call stressful? The master welcomes all challenges, people, events, and accidents. Their response is, "Everything is perfect; I just can't see it yet." To them, everything is a gift for which to be thankful.

The challenges they face are simply lessons that still need to be learned. They appreciate the opportunity to educate themselves further and to grow both intellectually and emotionally. They trust that the universe has a grand plan, and know they are not in control of the outcomes. They have seen the wisdom of infinite intelligence when a door is closed, and then a better opportunity ultimately presents itself.

They have learned to appreciate the little nuisances of life as well as simple pleasures. Major accomplishments are not as important as living in harmony and love. Acts of service are ways they show and receive appreciation. They understand there is no greater sacrifice than to offer someone else their precious time and attention.

They take time each day to acknowledge the gifts they have received and keep a daily gratitude journal. As they document and reflect on these things, they rekindle the feeling of love that comes from them. They appreciate the divine guidance that makes a fulfilled life possible and sweet. They accept misfortunes as welcome opportunities that are yet to be overcome.

TOTAL RESPONSIBILITY

Total responsibility is taking ownership of everything that happens in your life. This means all you have become you have created such as your health, your wealth, your relationships, your job, and your outlook on life. You have attracted everything and everyone into your life. Justifications, shame, and blame are not part of your thought process.

When mistakes happen, you don't waste time looking for who is responsible, because you already know. Instead, you immediately look for flaws in your processes or communications. As was stated before, "communication is the response I get." When things don't go as planned, it is often because the expectations and details were not sufficiently communicated to both sides.

Total responsibility keeps you in constant learning mode, so your energy is focused on making improvements in your behavior and processes instead of blaming others. You even expect to overcome the flaws and mistakes of others through better planning and design. You begin to anticipate and account for others' actions even when they are out of alignment with the goal.

Total responsibility acknowledges that over time you ultimately have control over almost everything. Therefore, you think over a longer term and find ways to influence yourself and others in the manner you desire. You put long-term plans into action and expand your social network until what you desire can be obtained. You make time your friend by using it to your advantage.

The gifts of total responsibility are certainty of success and growth. Others will beat a path to your door and offer you great opportunities to manage. Your ability to adapt and learn will be superior to all others, and your goals will never elude you. They will become almost trivial to accomplish.

VISION ACHIEVEMENT

Masters can be identified by the achievement of their personal vision. They have selected and committed to big, scary goals and been able to bring them into reality. Their vision may not be complete, but its creation has been materialized in a significant way that benefits the world and the visionary. People now recognize them as a leader in their area of expertise.

The hard work and strategies employed at the journeyman level now are bearing fruit. They have assembled a cohesive and talented team that works together to expand further the vision. Responsibility, praise, and wealth are shared amongst the group. Masters have been able to enrich themselves as well as others.

Their vision is making a positive contribution to the world. It is changing the lives of everyone connected to it. They have leveraged win-win, intellectual property, and other proven strategies for the rapid expansion of their vision and influence.

They have begun teaching and mentoring others in the process of creation, and they seek to pass forward what they have learned and experienced. They share their knowledge and ideas freely, as they know the path to success should be open to all that seek it. They serve as a light in the darkness.

They do not rest on their accomplishments. They are expanding their vision and are working to make it even grander and more beneficial. They see themselves as leaders in any area they choose to enter. They rise to the greatest of challenges.

EXCLUSIVE SELECTION OF INFLUENCES

The prime influences in your environment are friends, partners, and family members. For this reason, masters are highly selective of those with whom they associate or do business. Family relationships are cherished, but consistently negative people, friends, or extended family are encouraged to change or are placed on limited access. Conversely, masters expand access to those that offer new ideas and positive energy.

Masters are abnormally loyal to those that give more than they take. They are relationship focused above all else. They also are always looking to improve themselves and make the world a better place. They naturally gravitate to others with the same mindset, and making more time for these people does reduce time spent with those unwilling to change. This natural exclusive selection process is understood and championed by masters.

Exclusive selection is also practiced in the products they purchase, the food they eat, and the businesses they will consider for purchase or joint ventures. In all areas, they are guided by their values and principles. An entity must be in alignment for a mutually beneficial transaction to occur. This is true unless the master has decided to use his or her influence to redirect a misguided entity toward the greater good.

DISTRACTION MASTERY

Focus and persistence are supreme in the minds of masters, and they can hold their concentration for much longer than the average person. It is this single-minded focus on their desires that sets them apart. They can concentrate on their goals for days, months, and even years until they are accomplished.

This does not mean they are unable to perform many tasks at once, as they also have mastered time management. It means they can set priorities and organize tasks so that their desires are always near the top. They carve out time each day to make progress and stay in motion towards their goals. They do not allow distractions to sidetrack them.

Distractions are inevitable and must be dealt with accordingly. Masters have simple ways to handle them. They know that most distractions appear urgent, but are not. When an interruption arises during a time reserved for focusing on their goals, they will document the issue and then return to it later. Masters keep lists and have systems to track distracting issues.

They block out and protect their focused time above all else. They understand that even small distractions can be costly by taking them out of the creative mindset. It can take several minutes to hours to regain the concentration that can be lost to minor distractions.

The creative mind that can simultaneously access, hold, and understand many concepts of an issue at once, is most productive. This takes study and quiet contemplation to occur. Once in this state, the mind enters a zone of ultimate creativity and problem-solving. You then can fully conceive the interrelationships among issues. The longer you remain in this state, the better the outcomes. Once this state is lost, it is difficult to regain.

This is why distractions must be mastered and dealt with at other times. They are destructive to the process of creation. Focus is the key to accomplishing your goals. Masters have found ways to isolate themselves from distractions to achieve clear thinking.

Action Oriented

Masters have conquered the inner demons that previously prevented them from performing the actions required for success and goal achievement. After all, success in any project or endeavor is just finding a model that works, then executing the plan. They no longer have to waste time with the indecision that comes from fear, resistance, and anxiety because they already know they will be successful.

Having developed a self-concept that supports their future success, they find it easy to take action. It flows naturally, as they find new opportunities, meet new people, and set new goals. Masters are always setting new, higher, and more challenging goals. They find ordinary goals to be inadequate, so they don't waste time on any goal that does not scare them.

A goal that is not big enough to scare them provides no energy and excitement. Therefore, they are always looking to set goals in areas they have not yet mastered. This requires a constant mindset of learning, mistake making to gain knowledge, and then making corrections. Masters are easily bored when they are not in learning mode towards a goal.

They know that actions and mistakes are by far the best teachers. Their inclination is to choose a course of action, then watch the results. They can then refine their actions using the feedback mechanism that mistakes and experience bring them. Indecision within themselves and by their partners and teams is not tolerated.

They thrive on making decisions without complete information. They know that leaders must often make choices before all the facts can be known. To them, leadership is the prediction of future events and outcomes. To do this, they rely on theories that have a high-reliability rate, such as intellectual property and leverage.

Above all, they prize bold and aggressive action in any situation. They know there is magic in taking a risk backed by faith and commitment. Playing it safe is rarely the best course of action. They would rather be the disrupter than be entrenched in old ways of seeing the world. They welcome and embrace change and all the opportunities it brings.

Clarity of Thought

Clear and thorough thinking are master skills. Taking time to allow ideas to evolve fully and being able to anticipate possible future effects is a sign of wisdom. Forcing decisions before the actions are fully understood increases the chance of a mistake. Although mistakes are not unwelcome, the master has learned to use them strategically for task execution feedback. They rarely want to make mistakes on major objectives.

Clarity of thought comes from taking regular time alone to consider issues and to ensure alignment with their values. Courses of action that are out of alignment are discarded if they cannot be realigned. The perceived values of potential partners are also critical to any decision. Alliances must be based upon common values to be successful. When in doubt one must enter into a discussion of values.

Clarity of thought is best created in a place with few distractions. The mind must be given time to understand and hold multiple ideas and their interrelationships in the brain simultaneously. This allows the mind to model a concept and the potential outcomes entirely. Once interrupted, this process is very difficult to recreate.

Clarity of thought also comes from leveraging the thoughts and ideas of your team. Beyond values alignment, input gained through the diverse ideas of others will improve any decision. Leveraging a team in this way brings to the table many more ideas and perspectives. Plans can be vastly improved by leveraging diversity.

Snap decisions are often misguided ones. For that reason, an opportunity should be foregone instead of rushing into an agreement that has not been fully thought out. Special attention must be paid to the way any action feels. If it feels right, then moving forward is more likely. If it feels wrong, then do not proceed. Masters have learned to trust their instincts.

FIND JOY IN EVERYTHING

When we are mindful, joy can be found in every little thing we do and in every thought we think. There is positive energy gained by living in the now and having an appreciation for every opportunity or lesson. Masters have learned to choose their own perceptions of the world and how they feel about it. Did you know there is no intrinsic meaning other than what we assign to events? All meaning is assigned by people, and we can always choose to find joy.

As we have learned, many will place their happiness on hold while they wait for some future event to occur. They think they will be happy when this event happens or when they have that house or job or car. They end up withholding their appreciation of the world and living unhappily, lamenting what they lack instead of celebrating what they already have.

Masters have learned to live every day in appreciation. They live their dream life now regardless of their circumstances. They give thanks for their relationships and acts of service. They already have more than enough to achieve a fantastic life, and know living with excess is not necessary to be happy. They find joy in the wonders of nature, the dawn of a new day, a good friend, productive activities, a good meal, stretching, and using their bodies.

Choosing to live in joyfulness is simply a mindset and has nothing to do with your possessions or circumstances. Your life is already a dream filled with much for which to be thankful. Give yourself permission to be happy now, and you will lead the life of the master. True happiness is only a thought away.

GUIDANCE BY FAITH

What is it that guides most people's lives? There are many possibilities such as success, greed, lust, faith, fear, love, and scarcity. For many, fear has too much power. They will become slaves to their fears and end up being easily manipulated. Others are very focused on becoming rich, but for selfish reasons; they do not intend to do good works with their wealth. The master understands and welcomes wealth as a means to benefit the world.

Masters are guided by faith in themselves and the goodness of the universe. They seek the best not only for themselves; they seek the best for the world. They desire to be instruments of the universe performing tasks that benefit the greater good. They know they are not in control of the world but are mere participants in a mysterious grand design.

They have faith in the love and goodness of the world. They have faith in humanity and their abilities. They have faith that any project or goal that benefits the greater world can be successful. They refuse to be controlled by greed, fear, scarcity, and doubt. They avoid any organization that would utilize these tools to accomplish a task.

Instead, their faith guides them to act in love and support of others. They know there are only two ways to live—in fear or faith. By choosing to live in faith, they do not waste thoughts on loss or defeat. They recognize that bringing a negative thought into their minds is to bring it into the world. Instead, they bring only positive thoughts and ideas into their minds.

They believe that everything they do matters. There is not a single thought or action they make that does not have an effect on the world. To think or act with malice is to create malice. To think and act with love is to create love. Their thoughts and actions seek to be in alignment at all times.

Guidance by faith is bringing your inner world into your outer world. The inside materializes the outside. This is true manifestation in action.

CHAPTER SUMMARY

Master chosen ones have learned to overcome their limiting beliefs, distractions, the comfort zone, and the opinions of others. They have created a vision for their life that is guided by a higher purpose. They have recreated themselves, their relationships with others, and they have persistently worked until their vision has been achieved.

They have learned to master their inner life, the one within their mind. Having mastered their thoughts and learned to trust their feelings, they are capable of bringing their outer life into alignment. They believe in themselves and know that they are worthy of their dreams. They have developed powerful characteristics such as persistence, gratitude, love, and responsibility.

They developed a vision for themselves and the world and brought it into being. They changed their environment so that it supported them and their goals. They discovered and employed proven strategies that made their efforts effective. These same strategies have been used for centuries.

They disciplined themselves so that their habits and strategies worked in their favor. The habits of excellence, clear thought, and living in joy have served them well. They are guided by a faith that taps into the universal sources of creativity and knowledge, and once they aligned themselves with this powerful force, they became unstoppable.

As a review, the steps of the master are shown below.
1. High self-value and self-concept
2. Indifference to others opinions
3. Grateful for everything
4. Total responsibility
5. Vision achievement
6. Exclusive selection of influences

7. Distraction mastery
8. Action oriented
9. Clarity of thought
10. Find joy in everything
11. Guidance by faith

CLOSING

CONCLUSION

When you serve a higher purpose, you are
always in service of mankind. Being in service
of others is the way of the chosen ones.

There are powerful myths and distractions in the world today that seek to take away our personal power. They seduce us with thoughts of easy lives, easy money, and teach us to be victims and blame others for our failures. They set an example that leads us to believe that only a select group will succeed. Far too many have adopted this belief and live in despair.

However, a coming revolution will reverse this trend. The world is in desperate need of strong leaders and dreamers. There is a new realization that everyone has incredible talents and gifts and has already been chosen for greatness. The myth of the rare chosen one is a lie. All you need to become successful and to activate your gifts is to choose yourself for greatness and take action with persistence and belief. By choosing yourself, you will bring forth new sources of inner strength and personal belief. You become one of the real chosen ones who are rising up and fulfilling their destiny.

Having appointed yourself for greatness, you learned to walk the path of the chosen ones. You discovered the path begins at the level of the initiate and with time, skill, knowledge, and action anyone can become a master. By mastering your own thoughts, actions, and beliefs, you gain true alignment with your life's higher purpose. The creation of your new life begins to emerge.

In this book, you learned the myth that is taken as truth by many. You observed that the myth of the chosen one if believed, excludes you from greatness. You discovered there was no secret group that you must join to have success. You just need the strength and courage to choose yourself and become a star in your life.

The dynamics model and key concepts matrix showed you the essential components of a fully mastered life. The way they were linked together displayed that self-esteem and self-concept were at the root of all personal development. Belief in yourself is now recognized as the shining star in the center of your own solar system. The planets in your solar system all revolve around this and rely on it for their heat and energy. No solar system can exist without a powerful star at its core.

You learned how the planets of your solar system develop effective habits, refine your characteristics, change your environment, leverage strategies, create yourself, and connect with infinite intelligence. Each of these planets has many subcomponents that build upon each other and guide your personal development journey.

The attainment levels to become a master were laid out, and you now have a guide and roadmap to follow as you pursue a new, fantastic life. Each step in the process has key concepts required for success. You learned there is a hierarchy of the process and by proceeding one step at a time, you can easily master each one.

By overlaying the Dynamics Model and the Attainment Levels, you learned about the Key Concepts Matrix. You discovered a grand master is an expert at all levels and dynamics. You also saw that successful, focused masters do exist, but, if not careful, they have vulnerabilities that can destroy them.

You learned powerful business strategies employed by the most successful businesses and great thinkers. These concepts will magnify your actions, make each step more effective, and guarantee success. In this way, you now have the same knowledge as any captain of industry.

You also learned not to go in alone as a maverick. A small, dedicated team is a requirement for any business or project. You discovered a low percentage of something huge is always larger than 100% of very little.

When I started writing this book, it was not my intention to show others how to choose themselves for greatness or describe the five attainment levels. I did not yet understand the myth of the chosen one nor did I comprehend the progression of my personal development and how to tell others about it.

The original vision was to write a life lessons book for my children. Publishing my work was not even in my consciousness. However, over the course of my journey as a writer, new amazing thoughts, and ideas I never envisioned came into existence.

This book was inspired by my connection with infinite intelligence, persistence, and my desire for a framework to help describe my personal journey of growth and belief. It has evolved and grown into something very different and greater than I imagined.

The thoughts and ideas started from within me but soon took on a life of their own. At times, I just needed to allow the process to be revealed. It is proof that if you have the audacity to pursue and believe in a goal, the universe knows the best way to accomplish it and make it serve the most possible.

As my reader moving forward to become one of the many chosen ones, remember it is not selfish to enrich yourself as long as you also enrich others in the process. When you serve a higher purpose, you are always in service of humanity. Being in service to others is the way of the chosen ones. There is no higher goal than being of service. The more you serve, the more you will receive.

It has been my pleasure to serve you as a writer -- Namaste.

Acknowledgements

I want to thank my wife Kimberly whose love and support have always carried me. She is my best friend, the mother of our children, and my greatest cheerleader. She taught me the importance of emotional intelligence and innermost wisdom.

I am indebted to my teachers and mentors who made the content of this book possible. Marshall Thurber contributed many of the business strategies and taught me the importance of self-concept. Jane Willhite and PSI Seminars provided the personal development courses that helped me discover the importance of awareness and having a life vision.

Bob Proctor showed me the power of the subconscious mind. Nadine Lajoie, my mentor, and coach provided the steps and encouragement to bring this book to life. Rita Soman taught me PYSCH-K and how to access my inner child, and Jim Britt revealed the power of letting go of my past.

Finally, as a father, my desire to teach my two sons how to live a fulfilled life, a life with love, family, meaningful work, and abundance has never waned. This book is my way of giving them the lessons in life I wanted to teach and hoped to communicate fully.

About the Author

Joseph C. Parker is an author, radio host, cyber security expert, and the founder of PYL Radio, who lives in Washington State. He is a published co-author in *Here's How I Did It* (Stardom Books, 2014). He has an MBA from Seattle University. After spending 25 years in high technology, he set out to transform the media industry with ideas gained from PSYCH-K, PSI Seminars, Andy Dooley, Bob Proctor, and Burklyn Global. He can be found online at http://www.riseofthechosenones.com.

Joseph is a successful real estate investor and computer network security expert for the US Navy. He has built an extensive online business platform which includes several websites and social media networks. His weekly self-help blog is read by his subscriber list and is syndicated through Facebook, Twitter, LinkedIn, and Plurk.

He hosts the Program Your Life audio podcast with Kimberly Parker. The podcast interviews authors and speakers and is distributed on iTunes, Tunein.com, and Stitcher. He has featured speakers such as Nadine Lajoie, and Ernesto Sirolli.

PYL RADIO

Are you tired of all the negative information and music in the world? Are you ready for positive change in your life? Give PYL Radio a listen and tune in for inspirational lectures from top speakers for free, exclusive live shows, and positive music. Wake up to a soothing meditation instead of a buzzer. Stream it to all your smart devices...even your car.

http://www.programyourlife.org/

I created Program Your Life Radio (PYL Radio) so that everyone could have a daily stream of positive content to balance out the negative influences in the world. PYL provides free music and inspiring stories in streaming, Internet radio format. You can download songs from many of the artists for free, and the station constantly is adding new material. Artists can submit original audio material for airplay. The station now has listeners in more than 40 countries and still is growing.

PYL is a streaming Internet radio network that brings the best lectures, music, stories, meditations, and entertainment to the mobile platform. The radio network is fun and lively. We feature content from many speakers for which they normally charge. You can access this radio channel from virtually anywhere.

We now have a mobile app in the Google Play Store. Just search for "PYL Radio," download it today, and start listening. Living a balanced lifestyle on the go is easy with PYL Radio.

The PYL Podcast

Also, check out the Program Your Life Podcast, which is about overcoming obstacles, fears, and doubts in life. The hosts, Joe and Kimberly Parker, challenge themselves to pursuit their dreams and goals and share the journey of self-discovery along the way. The show is bound to be a rollercoaster ride with lots of fun, too. Each week the hosts discuss a topic and share what is working for them, as well as feature special guests who are making a positive difference in the world.

You can find the PYL podcast at www.programyourlife. org. It is also available on iTunes, DoubleTwist, Speaker, and Stitcher.

~

A GIFT FOR YOU

For several special bonus gifts and to download fully detailed copies of the Key Concepts Matrix go to the website http://www.riseofthechosenones.com/matrix

~∞~

Appendix
Quiz answers

Chosen One Quiz Answers

S – Choose the sentence that best describes you now
1. Success is inconvenient
    a. 2pts willing to make necessary sacrifices for success
2. Success is in my future
    a. 0pts not living in the now
3. Success takes commitment and work
    a. 0pts success is not really hard
4. Success is easy to me
    a. 1pt a positive attitude towards success

W – Choose the sentence that best describes you now
1. Other people deserve my best
    a. 0pts other people will accept you as you are
2. I talk kindly to myself
    a. 2pts shows self-love
3. I hold myself to a high personal standard
    a. 0pts too hard on yourself
4. I am always doing better
    a. 1pt it's good to be on the learning team

P – Choose the sentence that best describes you now
1. I am always getting better
    a. 2pts a person who is always growing
2. I always strive to be my very best
    a. 0pts a perfectionist view
3. People deserve only my best
    a. 0pts a perfectionist view
4. I cannot always do my best
    a. 1pt a realistic viewpoint

C – Choose the sentence that best describes you now
1. I like others to like me
   a. 0pts seeking outside approval
2. I like to be different than everyone else
   a. 2pts celebrating your uniqueness
3. I like to be the life of the party
   a. 0pts shows a need for attention
4. I like to be accepted by my peers
   a. 0pts seeking outside approval

M – Choose the sentence that best describes you now
1. It's important to visualize the end
   a. 1pt goal oriented
2. It's important to take steps
   a. 2pts action oriented
3. It's important to stay focused
   a. 0pts not action oriented
4. It's important to make sure I have the correct goal
   a. 0pts there are no correct goals

R – Choose the sentence that best describes you now
1. My choices are mostly good
   a. 1pt taking action and learning
2. I am like my parents
   a. 0pts a lack of personal choice
3. I am not a product of my environment
   a. 1pts taking responsibility for one's life
4. My environment has strongly shaped my life
   a. 0pts a lack of personal choice

G – Choose the sentence that best describes you now
1. I forgive but do not forget
    a. 0pts not full forgiveness
2. I protect myself from others who have hurt me
    a. 0pts a lack of forgiveness
3. I forgive so others feel better
    a. 1pts forgiveness but not the right reason
4. I forgive, so I feel better
    a. 2pts true forgiveness

M – Choose the sentence that best describes you now
1. I proceed carefully to do things correctly
    a. 0pts there is no correct way
2. I like to make mistakes
    a. 2pts the best way to learn
3. I make decisions quickly and occasionally fail
    a. 1pts a good attitude towards mistakes
4. I like to avoid mistakes
    a. 0pts a fear of making mistakes

S – Choose the sentence that best describes you now
1. I can usually tell what others think
    a. 0pts likes to make up stories about others
2. I anticipate what others think about me
    a. 0pts likes to make up stories about others
3. I don't know what others think
    a. 2pts a true statement
4. I can sometimes tell what others think
    a. 1pts some people have intuition

L- Choose the sentence that best describes you now
1. I am a leader of others
   a. 1pt shows leadership
2. I prefer to follow a strong leader
   a. 0pts a follower
3. I am a leader of myself
   a. 2pts true leadership
4. I am a reluctant leader
   a. 0pts a follower

I – Choose the sentence that best describes you now
1. I like to tie
   a. 1 pt a win-win attitude
2. I don't mind to lose
   a. 0pts a lose-win attitude
3. I like to win
   a. 0pts a lose-win attitude
4. I like to cooperate
   a. 2pts a true win-win attitude

V – Choose the sentence that best describes you now
1. I believe that others needs are more important than mine
   a. 0pts no self-value
2. I believe my needs are equal to others
   a. 1pt some self-value
3. I believe my needs must be met before considering other's needs
   a. 2pts true self-value
4. I believe that my needs are more important than others
   a. 0pts no self-value

F – Choose the sentence that best describes you now
1. Few fears are rational
   a. 2pts the true nature of fear
2. Fear is a necessary part of life
   a. 0pts living in fear
3. I prefer not to fear
   a. 0pts hiding from fear
4. There is no fear
   a. 1pt positive although somewhat reckless

E – Choose the sentence that best describes you now
1. I exercise when it's convenient
   a. 0pts a lack of discipline
2. I exercise on a calendar schedule
   a. 2pts shows commitment
3. I exercise rarely
   a. 0pts a lack of discipline
4. I exercise to feel better about myself
   a. 1pts a good attitude

CPSIA information can be obtained
at www.ICGtesting.com
Printed in the USA
BVOW08s0954131216
470646BV00001B/1/P